A Proust
SOUVENIR

Marcel Proust (1871–1922)

He was conscious of his charm and said that his eyes and complexion, together with the winning and attentive manner of a young, cherubic page, captivated the ladies. And he didn't conceal that he was a little in love with all of them too. It was natural, at his age, but I think a stronger reason still was the need to know he was able to please.

Céleste Alberet, *Monsieur Proust: A Memoir*

A Proust

SOUVENIR

William Howard Adams

Period Photographs by Paul Nadar

The Vendome Press · New York Paris

To Louis Auchincloss

Acknowledgment: Excerpts from REMEMBRANCE OF THINGS PAST, Volumes 1–3,
by Marcel Proust, translated by C.K. Scott Moncrieff and Terence Kilmartin.
Translation Copyright © 1981 by Random House, Inc. and Chatto & Windus Ltd.
Reprinted by permission of Random House, Inc.

Editor: Daniel Wheeler
Designer: Marlene Rothkin Vine

Copyright © 1984 The Vendome Press
First published in Great Britain by Weidenfeld & Nicolson
First published in the United States of America by
The Vendome Press, 515 Madison Avenue, N.Y., N.Y. 10022
Distributed by Rizzoli International Publications, 579 Fifth Avenue, New York, N.Y. 10017
Distributed in Canada by Methuen Publications

Library of Congress Cataloging in Publication Data
Adams, William Howard.
    A Proust souvenir.
      1. Proust, Marcel, 1871–1922—Friends and associates.
2. Proust, Marcel, 1871–1922—Characters. 3. France—
Biography. 4. Photography—Portraits. 5. Photography—
France—History.   I. Nadar, Paul, 1856–1939.   II. Title.
PQ2631.R63Z4612   1984   843'.912 (B)   84–7309

ISBN: 0-86565-042-X
Printed and bound in Italy

Acknowledgments

Since its first appearance, the English edition of Marcel Proust's novel À *La Recherche du temps perdu* has always been known as *Remembrance of Things Past*. For the present work I have used C.K. Scott Moncrieff's celebrated translation as revised by Terence Kilmartin and published in three volumes by Random House in 1981. Proust's original titles and their English equivalents are:

Du Côté de chez Swann (1913)
Swann's Way

À L'Ombre des jeunes filles en fleurs (1919)
Within a Budding Grove

Le Côté de Guermantes (1920–1921)
The Guermantes Way

Sodome et Gomorrhe I (1921), II (1922)
Cities of the Plain

Albertine disparue (1925)
The Fugitive

Le Temps retrouvé (1927)
Time Regained

Other books by Proust referred to in the text include *Les Plaisirs et les jours*, translated, under the title *Pleasures and Days*, by Louis Varèse, Gerard Hopkins, and Barbara Dupee (New York, 1957); *Jean Santeuil*, in Gerard Hopkins's translation (New York, 1957); *Contre Sainte-Beuve*, as rendered into English by Sylvia Townsend Warner and found in *Proust on Art and Literature: 1896–1919* (New York, 1956).

All admirers of Marcel Proust are very much in debt to Philip Kolb for his editing of the novelist's correspondence. A selection of the letters, translated by Ralph Mannheim with introductions by J.M. Cocking, is available in *Marcel Proust: Selected Letters: 1880–1903*. In the same year that Kolb's *La Correspondence générale de Marcel Proust* appeared (1949), Mina Curtiss brought out her translated edition of an important group of Proust letters, a volume cited here as *Letters*. In her later memoirs, *Other People's Letters*, Curtiss recounted her work on the correspondence and gave Proustiana one of its most charming books, spiced with unexpected adventures of Proust scholarship yielding some tiny particles of time regained.

The two-volume biography written by George Painter is the single most important source for background information on the large assemblage of Proustian personalities. Indeed, the present trifle could not have been done without the countless biographical details marshaled by Painter and presented in his great work. This and all other sources are fully documented in the notes found on page 126.

The complete manuscript was read by Katherine Mosby, who made many critical suggestions regarding both substance and style. The memory of our numerous discussions on various points remains one of the lasting pleasures that have accrued to me from my work on *A Proust Souvenir*. I am also grateful to Olivier Bernier, Mary Sargent d'Anglejan, and Philip Lyman for their advice and assistance.

All of the Nadar photographs have been made available for this project by courtesy of the Service des Archives de la Caisse Nationale des Monuments Historiques et des Sites. At the Service I particularly want to acknowledge the cooperation and patience of Geneviève Gareau and her staff. Most of the photographs appeared in an exhibition entitled *Le Monde de Proust*, as well as in a related catalogue prepared by Anne-Marie Bernard and Agnès Blondel. It was Gerald Incandela, however, who first brought Nadar's society portraits to my attention.

W.H.A.

Contents

Acknowledgments 5

Introduction 7

Swann's Way

Mme Adrien Proust *21* /   Robert Proust *24* /
Mme Émile Straus *(Duchesse de Guermantes, Odette)* *26* /
Charles Haas *(Swann)* *29* /   Gabriel Hanotaux *(Norpois)* *31* /
Mme Aubernon de Nerville *(Mme Verdurin)*   Dr. Samuel Pozzi *(Cottard)* *34* /
Professor Georges Dieulafoy *37* /   Madeleine Lemaire *(Mme Verdurin)* *38* /
Camille Barrère *(Norpois)* *40* /   Reynaldo Hahn *43* /
Jean Pouquet *(Gilberte)* *44* /   Willie Heath *47* /   Laure Hayman *(Odette)* *48* /
Nicolas Cottin *50* /   Alfred Agostinelli *(Albertine)* *52* /

The Guermantes Way

Marie de Benardaky *(Gilberte)* *57* /   Mme de Benardaky *(Odette)* *58* /
Lt. Comte Armand de Cholet *(Saint-Loup)* *60* /
Comtesse Élisabeth Greffulhe *(Duchesse and Princesse de Guermantes)* *62* /
Comtesse Laure de Chevigné *(Duchesse de Guermantes)* *65* /
Duc Armand de Guiche *(Saint-Loup)* *66* /
Marquis Boni de Castellane *(Saint-Loup)* *68* /
Marquise Boni de Castellane *(née Anna Gould)* *70* /
Vicomte Robert d'Humières *(Saint-Loup)* *71* /   Comtesse de Martel *(Gilberte)* *72* /
Comte Henri Greffulhe *(Duc de Guermantes)* *75* /
Comte Robert de Montesquiou *(Charlus)* *76* /
Prince Boson de Sagan *(Charlus)* *79* /
Comte Louis de Turenne *(Bréauté)* *80* /   Costume Ball of the Princesse de Leon *81* /
Marquise de Brantes *84* /   Princesse Mathilde *85* /
Edward, Prince of Wales *86* /   Princesse Hélène Soutzo *89* /
Prince Constantin Radziwill *(Prince de Guermantes)* *90* /
General Marquis Gaston de Galliffet *(Général de Froberville)* *92* /
Princesse Alexandre Bibesco *94* /

The Artists' and Writers' Way

Paul Desjardins *97* /   Alphonse Daudet *98* /   Anatole France *(Bergotte)* *101* /
Claude Monet *(Elstir)* *102* /   Gabriel Fauré *(Vinteuil)* *104* /
Claude Debussy *(Vinteuil)* *107* /   Édouard Risler *108* /   Marie de Heredia *109* /
Réjane *(Berma)* *110* /   Sarah Bernhardt *(Berma)* *113* /   Gaston Calmette *114* /
Louisa de Mornand *(Rachel)* *116* /   Méry Laurent *(Odette)* *119* /
Julia Bartet *120* /   Lucie Delarue-Mardus *121* /
Cora Laparcerie *122* /   Paul Nadar *124* /

Notes *126*

Index *127*

Introduction

❛. . . large birds flew swiftly over the Bois, as over a real wood, and with shrill cries perched, one after another, on the great oaks which, beneath their Druidical crown, and with Dodonian majesty, seemed to proclaim the unpeopled vacancy of this deconsecrated forest, and helped me to understand how paradoxical it is to seek in reality for the pictures that are stored in one's memory, which must inevitably lose the charm that comes to them from memory itself and from their not being apprehended by the senses. . . .❜

From the conclusion to *Swann's Way*

Proust the dissembler was almost as artful as his Narrator in *Remembrance of Things Past*. George Painter has compiled an astounding census of over one hundred fifty of the author's contemporaries from among the characters in the novel; yet for all of his intense, professional interest in people and, especially, his circle of friends—observing, studying, collecting, verifying, comparing his specimens with the obsession of a scientist—Proust was careful never to give his game away. "There are no keys to the people in my novel," he once claimed. Then, to confuse the matter further and to cover his tracks, he explained: "Or rather there are eight or ten keys to each character." The last Queen of Naples had no doubt about one key when, shortly after Proust's death, she found herself described in *The Captive*. The shock of recognition was instant. "It's odd, I never knew this Proust," she declared, "but he seems to know me very well, because he has made me act precisely as I think I would have done."[1]

Suspicious clues began to inspire debate and speculation even while Proust lived; later, of course, they proved irresistible to scholars sorting out the sources hidden behind an extraordinary array of Proustian personalities. Once identified, some of the friends, acquaintances, or enemies would consider it a dubious thing indeed to have had such immortality bestowed upon them. The gift might be in return for nothing more than the contribution of a soiled detail to a minor or unappealing character, as in the case of Mlle Vinteuil and her lesbian liaisons. An obscure cocotte, Liane de Pougy, who happened to be the mistress of a friend of Proust's father, has, for example, been detected in the behavior of the composer's daughter, a discovery not likely to change the course of Proust studies. Still, the revelation exemplifies the thoroughness that *Remembrance of Things Past* has provoked in certain aspects of scholarly research, almost from the moment the first chapters appeared. Then especially it posed considerable risk for those recognized in some facet of a personality or some set of actual events, since the opening sections of the great novel presented a mine field of surprises, often with bizarre twists, in the complex development of such major characters as Swann, Gilberte, or Charlus. Suppose, for instance, that as the narrative unfolded people suddenly thought they had discovered themselves or a close friend in one of the fictional characters. But picture their subsequent consternation when that character revealed an embarrassing vice or manners betraying a social background somewhat below the level first suggested. After all, as Proust told his friend Mme Straus, "if one of my characters turns out to poison people or commit incest later on, they will think I mean them!"

Some of his more discerning friends immediately suspected what Proust was up to and, seeing through the closet "entomologist," often confronted him with their own conclusions about who was who in his collection of specimens. Usually, the author would deny any connection and dismiss as mere coincidence telltale signs that seemed to point toward some obvious candidate. Nevertheless, Robert de Montesquiou had no difficulty recognizing himself in the character of Baron de Charlus, and he was outraged. Proust later told his housekeeper Céleste Albaret that Montesquiou had come at him like a caged lion, and that it had required all his charm and powers of persuasion to convince the offended grandee that he was wrong. Among other things, the novelist cited the fact that Charlus was much shorter! Although Proust was a young man when he met Montesquiou and had been fascinated by the Baron's elegance and arrogant manners, Céleste insisted that he maintained the friendship only long enough to complete his research. "As in all other cases," Céleste recalled, "once he had stored up all he needed for his Charlus, he severed relations. While he still needed to study the character, he observed his every step."[2]

When it came to such characters as Swann, the portrait proved so transparent that no friend of Charles Haas's had to wait for Proust's confession, which finally appeared in *The Captive*, to discover who had been the living model. Mme Straus had dubbed him Swann-Haas after the first reading of *Remembrance of Things Past*. "If, in Tissot's picture representing the balcony of the Rue Royale Club," Proust wrote, "where you figure with Galliffet, Edmond de Polignac, and Saint-Maurice, people are always drawing attention to you, it is because they know that there are some traces of you in Swann." Proust also left no doubt about his own awareness that he was bestowing a certain immortality on Haas and others whom he had appropriated for his work. In a dedicatory passage to Haas, also in *The Captive*, the novelist speaks candidly of his indebtedness: "And yet, my dear Charles, whom I used to know when I was still young and you were nearing your grave, it is because he whom you must have regarded as a young idiot has made you the hero of one of his novels that people are beginning to speak of you again and that your name will perhaps live."[3]

Quite apart from his genius as a writer, Marcel Proust possessed such an extraordinary and eccentric personality that it would be sufficient to make him and his more flamboyant friends the subjects of considerable biographical interest. Even his birth in 1871 within weeks of *La Semaine Sanglante*, the "Bloody Week" in May during which the revolutionary Commune was suppressed, provided a dramatically appropriate beginning. For the novelist obsessed with a society that seemed to have collapsed, only to engineer its own miraculous revival and thorough metamorphosis, the brief but violent convulsion in the spring of 1871 expressed the social and political uncertainties that would continue to quiver just below the surface of Proust's hothouse world—the world of *La Belle Époque*.

In this aftermath of the Franco-Prussian War, it was clearly not a spring to be in Paris. Having survived a ghastly winter and the German siege, Dr. Adrien Proust finally took his pregnant young wife of nine months—they had been married only two days after that dark moment in French history when Napoleon III's army surrendered at Sédan—to a safe retreat in nearby Auteuil. There, in his Uncle Louis Weil's house, Marcel Proust was born on June 10, 1871.

The condition of the baby was so fragile that his christening was delayed for several weeks. Proust later attributed the delicate health that plagued him throughout his life to the hardships suffered by his mother during the desperate months before he was born.

The city of Paris had indeed passed through a terrible ordeal, a civil war that even now is scarcely imaginable, so effective were the efforts of the survivors to cover up and forget, or at least to distance, the bitter reality of defeat. Two weeks before Marcel's birth, Edmond de Goncourt had watched from a Parisian rooftop while an ominous white cloud spread over the capital. As he noted in his diary, Goncourt was also unnerved that day by a deadly silence, a silence signaling the beginning of the end as the troops of the French government, now exiled in Versailles, began to stalk their prey, the Communard rebels.

The Prousts themselves had escaped just in time to miss the street fighting that erupted in their district. "This morning we were surrounded by National Guards," reported a neighbor who stayed behind. "We heard fusillades in the direction of the Faubourg Saint-Honoré and the Champs-Élysées. After a while the fight was so close to Saint-Augustin, in the Boulevard Malesherbes, and at last the soldiers reached our street. We could not even put our nose through the window without risk of being struck by a ball."[4]

As the intensity of the last-ditch struggle grew, even suburbs like Passy and Auteuil were battered by shelling. In late May, Edmond de Goncourt made it to Auteuil, where he found his house pocked with shell fragments but still standing, whereas other structures nearby had been flattened. The lawn in his garden had grown rank "like an abandoned cemetery, with the shining leaves of its shrubs covered by plaster and black charred paper, with big branches broken off so that the brownish foliage of a dead tree is mingled with the green foliage of a living tree, with a big hole in the very middle . . . a hole big enough to bury three men in."[5]

The entire city, in fact, was being turned into a burial ground. Entries in the municipal account books for that spring record the payments for the disposal of more than seventeen thousand corpses before the fighting was over and life re-established in its old routines. "Pose" rather than "routine" may be a more appropriate word, for while appearances suggested a degree of order, the atmosphere vibrated with the uncertainties of a world riven by bitter enmities. "All is overpowered and spoiled by the mania for pose," an English visitor reported, "pose in literature, pose in religion, pose in love, pose even in great affections." In each of their major epochs the French had made theatrics and a keen sense of the stage one of the defining qualities of their culture, and as the nineteenth century moved through its last decades, they once again turned to public spectacle—elaborate sets, costumes, brilliant casts, appropriate music—to provide a baroque transition from one period to the next.

This was the Belle Époque, the glitter and style of whose great balls, receptions, exhibitions, and grand entrances at the Opéra—as well as its more intimate dinners, salons, and drawing-room histrionics (or intrigues)—supplied the backdrop for Proust's imagination. When the interlude was nearing its end just before World War I, the novelist would retreat to his cork-lined bedroom and there re-create that era and his own past in a work of art.

The Paris of Proust and La Belle Époque had its roots in the smoking ruins of the Tuileries Palace, the Hôtel de Ville, the Palace of the Legion of Honor, and the Conseil d'État, all destroyed in 1871, but we would be hard put to know it from Proust's conversations, letters, and writing, which seldom refer to the implications of that disaster. The death rattles heard only days before Marcel Proust was born seemed to melt away in soft, impartial sounds, echoing down the quickly replanted avenues and boulevards of the Faubourg Saint-Germain, once again thronged with the fine turn-outs of the Parisian *haut monde*. The speed with which order was restored reflected the desperate policy of government and the private agreement of society to hide their inner weakness behind a screen of shimmering display. Splendid new houses and public monuments replaced the old ones (all but the decrepit Tuileries Palace) and became the setting for spectacles without number. Young Henry James reported in the *New York Tribune* that Paris was attempting, and rightly so, to recover her composure and self-esteem by mounting gala productions in Garnier's new temple dedicated to Musical Drama, better known as the Paris Opéra. Perhaps a trifle vulgar, and certainly theatrical, yet the effect on a temporarily confused and demoralized society seemed to be the very tonic needed to help the French capital regain its celebrated poise and tranquility.

The Grand Illusion (some thought it a clumsy accident) called the Third Republic, with its revived social sheen, its new fortunes and international exhibitions, its frantic faith in engineered Progress, the latter symbolized by Eiffel's giant "Erector Set" tower, helped to deaden memories of the recent devastations. "I continued to go to the Champs-Élysées on fine days, along streets whose elegant pink houses seemed to be washed (because exhibitions of water-colours were then the height of fashion) in a lightly floating atmosphere," the Narrator recalls in a passage celebrating the "New Paris" over the old Paris, which had been eclipsed and reduced by shabby comparison with its dazzling, parvenu neighbors. "It would be untrue to say that in those days the palaces of Gabriel struck me as being of greater beauty than, or even of another period from, the neighbouring houses. I found more style and should have supposed more antiquity if not in the Palais de l'Industrie at any rate in the Trocadéro. . . . Once only one of Gabriel's palaces made me stop for more than a moment; this was because, night having fallen, its columns dematerialized by the moonlight had the appearance of having been cut out in pasteboard, and by reminding me of a set from the operetta *Orphée aux enfers*, gave me for the first time an impression of beauty."[6]

That Gabriel's Place de la Concorde should be reduced in the Narrator's eye to a stage-set for an Offenbach operetta seems compatible with the effort to conceal the ugly realities lurking behind the fantasies of *fin-de-siècle* Paris, fantasies indulged in by the mannered aristocracy and the moralistic bourgeoisie alike. By conveying, with his extraordinary subtlety, the concrete sense of things—buildings, furniture, places—where all seemed expendable, Proust manages at the same time to endow his world with the fascination of a curious unreality. It is this anomaly that transfixes us when the Narrator speaks of the birds flying "swiftly over the Bois, as over a real wood" and recalls how their "shrill cries . . . helped me to understand how paradoxical it is to seek in reality for the pictures that are stored in one's memory. . . ."[7]

Throughout his life Proust would be preoccupied with the tensions between appearances and reality, with the paradox of illusions, created by jewels, gestures, titles, names, ways of speaking, and the deeper truths overlaid by all those beguiling appurtenances. He would never outgrow that childlike wonder "when the world has not yet become something completely known and real, when it seems that an unfamiliar place in the real world might well give access to the world of the unreal." With these words Howard Moss concluded his critical study of *Remembrance of Things Past*, a study in which he described Proust as "the greatest disenchanter" because he "was so greatly enchanted." However brief, the summation helps us to grasp the special magic of the novel's language.[8]

Throughout the Belle Époque, from the last two decades of the old century to the end of the first decade of the new one, the members of Paris's established order redoubled, without acknowledging, their efforts (efforts that Proust no doubt sensed at an early age) to maintain at least the semblance of decorum in their lives. Nowhere did Proust express his acute awareness of the fragility of those pervasive illusions than in his description of "the crack of a cat-o-nine-tails, for it was followed by the cries of pain" from the Baron de Charlus, wracked by excruciating pleasure as he submits, slave-like, to the lashes applied by his hired "dominator," Maurice.[9] It is the penultimate horror scene in the novel, and by its very intensity the shocking disclosure of the degradation sought by a leading member of Faubourg society illuminates an awful truth hidden behind the theater sets so hastily designed and thrown up by that society.

"Without some knowledge of Proust's biography," Roger Shattuck has written, "we would remain blind to a whole section of countryside surrounding his world and lending meaning to it."[10] Peopling that "countryside" (or rather "cityscape" since it is Paris that mainly concerns us here) are the men and women whom Proust included in his wide circle of friends and who were also the clients of the photography studio founded by Félix Nadar during the Second Empire. As we read the extraordinary roster of names that figured in Nadar's appointment schedule and discover their Proustian connections, it is as if the writer himself had conspired with the photographer, for the benefit of posterity, to record the faces of his world so that we can understand the raw material from which he drew inspiration for the great novel.

One of the undoubted classics of the twentieth century, *Remembrance of Things Past* appeared, volume by volume, from 1913 through 1927 until it totalled over three thousand pages. Treating the evolution of the novel as an extension of his life, Proust claimed that the earliest sections incorporated compositions he had written at the age of fourteen. Numerous portions of the novel were, in fact, derived from previous writings and short sketches that the author transposed into the main body of the work. Quoting Keats, to the effect that a man's life is a continual allegory, George Painter concluded that *Remembrance of Things Past* "is the allegory of Proust's life, a work not of fiction but of imagination interpreting reality."[11] The view is one that becomes ever more persuasive as we extend our knowledge of both that life and its work.

Even at a very young age, Proust seems to have been aware of his special gifts, if not the exact purpose to which he would put them. The son of a distinguished doctor and a beloved mother from a family of successful Jewish stockbrokers, young Marcel knew that with his soft, semitic good looks and gentle manners he could easily please and manipulate people. It was not long before he also realized that his precocious ways could serve as a passport out of the bourgeois "club" where he had been born and into that other "club" where he felt drawn. The Duchesse de Clermont-Tonnerre got it right when she said that Proust was "simply born in one circle and fell in love with another. It was like two clubs ... each equally good in its own way, but no one then belonged to both."[12] By exercising his undeniable charm and attaching himself to wealthy and aristocratic classmates at the Lycée Condorcet, Proust succeeded in moving into the most important literary, artistic, and social salons of Paris, the "club" he aspired to as an artist-in-the-making.

One of the first salons into which Proust ventured was the bourgeois but cultivated drawing room of Mme Arman de Caillavet, where he first met the celebrated French writer Anatole France, the hostess's aging lover. It was a good beginning, and other invitations would quickly follow. One of them came from Mme Émile Straus, who introduced young Proust to Mme de Clermont-Tonnerre, a denizen of that *quartier noble* known since the Middle Ages as the Faubourg Saint-Germain. The Duchesse de Clermont-Tonnerre was the daughter of the Duc de Gramont, head of one of France's oldest, most aristocratic families and the bearer of a name that would be freighted with such history and meaning for Proust in his explorations into the higher reaches of society. Mme de Clermont-Tonnerre was also discovering a new world, albeit from a totally different perspective, and her first impression conveys a glimpse of the social stratification prevailing at the time:

It was at Mme de Caillavet's, in the circle where Anatole France lived and thought, that I first became aware of the astonishing diversity of the compartments into which most French people shut themselves. The rather scandalized surprise my presence and M. de Clermont-Tonnerre's evoked in the salon of the Avenue Hoche stupefied me. What secret, terrible reasons were there to make a young couple swap polo and the races for the Caillavet Sundays? ... For me the idea of seeing, of listening to the author of Le Lys rouge, L'Étui de nacre, La Rôtisserie de la Reine Pédauque was not natural. ... I thought of Anatole France as an abstraction, as remote as Buddha, Plato or Renan. He was a mythical figure everyone talked about, whose books everyone read but who unlike everyone else couldn't sit down in an armchair, lunch with his neighbors, receive money from his publishers, buy a hat or yawn behind a newspaper.[13]

The magnetic pull that Proust felt toward this fashionable, rarefied, mysterious world has given him and his novel a reputation for snobbery. Some readers even take the book to be merely an autobiography written by a wealthy, coddled boy who grew up on the fringes of the high society he worshiped and longed to join. But this is a superficial reading, one that is not borne out by the actual masterpiece that would begin to emerge between 1905 and 1909, when Proust the eccentric man-about-town became a dedicated man of letters with a clear vision of his life's work set out before him. Over the next fifteen years, after abruptly withdrawing from society and crawling into his famous bed, he proceeded to re-create the world he had studied and now left behind him. By doing so imaginatively and with all the genius that was uniquely his, he realized an artistic monument of timeless significance.

A devastating social satire, as merciless and funny as any ever written, *Remembrance of Things Past* describes and probes to its very roots the pretensions of an ancient civilization undergoing irremediable changes at every level. Its members play out their comic and tragic, though seldom understood, roles, moving from one to the other in the same line or breath. Only a subtle shift in the rhythm or gesture signals the altered condition of things. "It is not," as Mme de Clermont-Tonnerre has written, "a story you hurry through to discover the unwinding of the plot. It is a miraculous promenade reaching from the earth to the heavens and descending to the depths of the sea. A reader who opens one of the ten volumes of *À La Recherche du temps perdu* will find himself in contact with the human flux."[14]

Photographs and particularly photographic portraits from the period help us to organize and to penetrate at least the surface of that flux. They are like mirrors held up to an age, and with their reflected imagery we are much better able, almost a century later, to revisualize the life and society that inspired the novel. While most of the photographs associated with Proust were taken by Paul Nadar, or under his direction, the studio founded by his father Félix Nadar stretched back to the early 1850s, a span of time that, with all its triumphs and tumult, fascinated Proust, for it was the foundation of his own immediate past. Nadar *père* had witnessed the advent of photography virtually from its inception, and in his exuberant involvement with the medium, he managed to discover and exploit most of its fundamental characteristics.

In the parade of faces recorded by the Nadar studio there are many that were either fashionable or well known both before and after the collapse of the Second Empire. Félix Nadar had started out as a journalist and caricaturist, producing a pictorial compendium of a thousand lithographed caricatures of the celebrities of mid-nineteenth-century Paris. The series was a big success, and with the earnings it generated Nadar set up his photography studio during the winter of 1854–55.

Gregarious, hospitable, bohemian, Félix Nadar soon attracted an impressive following. "There was always an open table at Nadar's," one of his assistants later recalled. "Alexandre [Dumas] would be rubbing shoulders with Offenbach, Sardou sitting next to Gustave Doré and actors from the Comédie Française next to Rochefort. Between the poses there would be fencing. There was always a noble clash of arms in the huge studio.... I was there the famous evening when he asked Offenbach to play 'La Marseillaise.' And Offenbach did so with all the windows open, ornamenting it with such fantastic virtuosity that even the imperial police could not stop him."[15]

Félix Nadar embellished his career with such well-publicized antics as his photographic adventures in a balloon that gave aerial photography a boost. Meanwhile, he had already taken his camera into the depths of the city, probing the urban underworld of sewers and catacombs, where he experimented with primitive artificial lighting in the form of galvanic arcs.

When Paul Nadar followed his father into the photographic business he brought to it a personality and a professional approach quite distinct from those of the elder Nadar, an old-fashioned bohemian who would often greet his clients dressed in a long crimson robe that set off his flaming red hair. By the time Paul took over the Nadar atelier in the early 1880s, the period when Marcel and his brother Robert went there for their first photographs, Félix had retreated to the countryside in semiretirement. Paul quickly replaced his father's creative, irreverent, anti-establishment reputation with a new bourgeois image of the well-dressed, soberly correct entrepreneur.

Paul Nadar may have lacked his father's self-assurance, but his efforts to ingratiate himself with the more exclusive members of Parisian society seem to have paid off. This becomes evident when we consider the social credentials of many of his sitters, among whom figured most of Proust's friends and new acquaintances in both the fashionable artistic world and the patrician enclave of the Faubourg Saint-Germain.

Proust's mother was of the generation for whom photography presented a great novelty. No doubt it was Mme Proust who had seen to it that every member of her family, including her busy husband, submitted to a session before the camera. But she believed, like many others of her class, that photographs were a private matter and not for public display. To show or give strangers a photograph of one's family or friends was to risk an invasion of privacy, revealing perhaps more than any stranger had the right to know. Even the presentation of one's photographic portrait to a friend entailed a special etiquette. Proust reminded Montesquiou that he should deliver his picture by hand, rather than trust it to the impersonal mails, for, as the novelist said, "one doesn't send photographs by post."[16]

Mina Curtiss, during her research of Proust's correspondence, recalled seeing a letter in which Mme Proust admonishes her son never to display a particular photograph of himself and two friends. The photograph, which had disturbed her, is the now well-known one where a cynical, mustachioed Marcel, wearing a bow tie and a boutonniere, is seated in front of two young admirers, Robert de Flers and Lucien Daudet. It may have been the latter's intense gaze at Proust and his effete gesture of resting an arm on the novelist's shoulder that caused Mme Proust to be concerned, arousing fears that the picture disclosed more than she cared to admit or have others discover.

Photographs figure in a number of places in *Remembrance of Things Past*. There is, for example, the scene in which Swann contemplates the recent changes Odette has undergone—"she was putting on weight and the expressive, sorrowful charm, the surprised wistful expression of old seemed to have vanished from her youth"—and studies a photograph to recall her former self: "Then he would look at photographs of her taken two years before, and would remember how exquisite she had been. And that would console him a little for all the agony he suffered on her account."[17] In *Within a Budding Grove* Charlus speaks of the special importance of photographs for the preservation of an unsullied moment of Time Past, before it had been altered by an indifferent present. He recalls a visit to the royal château at Blois, the home of his ancestors, where a caretaker boasted that he stored his brooms in Mary Stuart's private chapel. The horrified Baron is now forced to keep only "a photograph of the house, taken before it was unspoiled.... A photograph acquires something of the dignity which it ordinarily lacks when it ceases to be a reproduction of reality and shows us things that no longer exist."[18]

The sexual role of a photograph comes forward when Mlle Vinteuil desecrates her father's memory by placing a picture of the composer on a table in her bedroom so that it stands in full view of her lesbian ardors. In another episode, the suggestive photograph of an actress turns up among the possessions of the Narrator's deceased great-uncle and subsequently becomes the source for Elstir's sketch of Odette *en travesti*, a passage that further emphasizes the sexual mystique of photographs. For, as Proust and everyone else understood, the new technology had from the very beginning served an underground purpose, and its notorious function in the dissemination of pornographic images was tolerated by all levels of society. This modern phenomenon, with its subtle psychological dimensions, was grasped by Proust the novelist, who used photographs in the story in precisely the same way that he exploited the new technology of trains, cars, and airplanes as symbols of passing time.

Proust collected and treasured the photographs of his friends, giving his own in exchange on numerous occasions. While in the army, he took such pride in discovering his new role as a soldier that he once took pictures of his uniformed self to a dance and passed them out to friends. Céleste recalled in her memoirs the chest-of-drawers filled with photographs "of his mother and of friends and of relations but also of women he'd known and sometimes admired. . . . He often asked me to get them out for him. But it was chiefly in his memory that he rummaged. Then you could see that his thoughts were following a kind of underground track, as if he were organizing everything into images before putting them into words. His eyes became motionless, and I said nothing waiting for him to return from his internal journey."[19]

No doubt Proust used his collection of photographs to recall, in the course of his work on the novel, the images of particular personalities or the details of some costume or plumage. After he had virtually retired from society to devote himself totally to writing, Proust would occasionally emerge from seclusion and briefly attend some social affair where he could study an aspect of face or behavior he had forgotten, as if returning, like a painter, to recapture the light and shadow of a landscape he had neglected to sketch. In 1912 the novelist unexpectedly appeared at the last soirée of the season given by the Duchesse de Guiche in order once more to see, however fleetingly, the beautiful eyes of Mme Greffulhe, as well as "to refresh my memory of people's faces." The Comtesse Greffulhe's repeated refusal to give him her photograph may have provided a purely professional reason for his having accepted this one invitation.

Like the misleading use of the name Marcel for that of the Narrator, who, moreover, speaks in the first person, Proust's appropriation of recognizable people and places compounds the deceptions within the novel. In the end, Proust of course fashioned the epic story out of his own imagination, but like all great novelists—William Faulkner in Mississippi comes immediately to mind—he used biographical and physical details drawn from the only society he knew or could imagine. That Mme Greffulhe was, in fact, a great beauty whom the novelist saw and admired adds little to our ultimate understanding of the novel or the author's intentions. But her photographic representation fascinates us as a connection between the reality of a particular personality and its transformation in a work of art.

Proust actually denied that he used Mme Greffulhe as a source for more than a few lines of descriptive color in a passage devoted to the Duchesse de Guermantes. "I agree that during two minutes of Guermantes I," he wrote to his friend the Duc de Guiche in 1922, "there was a sparkle of dress and beauty at the Opéra which certainly had something of Madame Greffulhe. But not dreaming that a reader would pay attention to the detail of a book, I forgot to say that Madame de Guermantes, who in the course of five lines resembles Madame Greffulhe, is in no way the Duchesse de Guermantes in the salon which is so spoken of throughout an entire volume but her cousin, Princesse de Guermantes."[20] In a sense he was being truthful, for the portraits of the Guermantes ladies is a composite made from several of the Belle Époque's more glamorous personalities. Indeed, the famous meditation on the veiled goddess-like Duchesse, as the Narrator observes her in her box (actually the Greffulhe box) from his place in the orchestra, runs on for several pages. The later insistence by Proust that he had looked to the Comtesse Greffulhe only for her "sparkle of dress and beauty" can be weighed against the celebrated passage itself in order to appreciate the degree to which the artist penetrated the illusions of reality by his brilliant conflation of details observed in several different individuals:

❛Just as the curtain was rising on this second play I looked up at Mme de Guermantes's box. The Princess, with a movement that called into being an exquisite line which my mind pursued into the void, had just turned her head towards the back of her box; the guests were all on their feet, and also turned towards the door, and between the double hedge which they thus formed, with all the triumphant assurance, the grandeur of the goddess that she was, but with an unwonted meekness due to her feigned and smiling embarrassment at arriving so late and making everyone get up in the middle of the performance, the Duchess de Guermantes entered, enveloped in white chiffon. She went straight up to her cousin, made a deep curtsey to a young man with fair hair who was seated in the front row, and turning towards the amphibian monsters floating in the recesses of the cavern, gave to these demi-gods of the Jockey Club—who at that moment, and among them all M. de Palancy, in particular, were the men I should most have liked to be—the familiar "good evening" of an old friend, an allusion to her day-to-day relations with them during the last fifteen years. I sensed but could not decipher the mystery of that smiling gaze which she addressed to her friends, in the azure brilliance with which it glowed while she surrendered her hand to them one after another, a gaze which, could I have broken up its prism, analysed its crystallisations, might perhaps have revealed to me the essence of the unknown life which was apparent in it at that moment. . . . It was as though the Duchess had guessed that her cousin, of whom, it was rumoured, she was inclined to make fun for what she called her "exaggerations" (a noun which, from her point of view, so wittily French and restrained, was instantly applicable to the poetry and enthusiasm of the Teuton), would be wearing this evening one of those costumes in which the Duchess considered her "dressed up," and that she had decided to give her a lesson in good taste. Instead of the wonderful downy plumage which descended from the crown of the Princess's head to her throat, instead of her net of shells and pearls, the Duchess wore in her hair only a simple aigrette which, surmounting her arched nose and prominent eyes, reminded one of the crest on the head of a bird. Her neck and shoulders emerged from a drift of snow-white chiffon, against which fluttered a swansdown fan, but below this her gown, the bodice of which had for its sole ornament innumerable spangles (either little sticks and beads of metal, or brilliants), moulded her figure with a precision that was positively British. But different as their two costumes were, after the Princess had given her cousin the chair in which she herself had previously been sitting, they could be seen turning to gaze at one another in mutual appreciation.❜[21]

One of the distinguishing characteristics of the novel, as opposed, for example, to the fable, the romance, or the fairy tale is its concern with reality. For all their differences in style and formal point of view, Jane Austen, Dickens, Balzac, Tolstoy, Melville, Faulkner, and Joyce meet on common ground in their commitment to an actual, real, verifiable world.

No matter how one may go about concocting a definition of the novel, "the staple ingredient," Mary McCarthy has remarked, "in fairly heavy dosages is fact." Not only in the rich, knowing detail but in the sheer gross bulk of *Remembrance of Things Past*, Proust built up those layers of facts, those kaleidoscopic scenes that are so essential to the visualization and understanding of each character. Through description and through highlighting as carefully orchestrated as that of a great film director, Proust made his portraits of Mme de Guermantes, Baron de Charlus, Mme Verdurin, Saint-Loup unforgettable for the very good reason that he brought them to life as real people in a world of his own creation.

Even such a minor character as Legrandin the engineer has been filtered through Proust's prism of observation and skillfully rendered with a particularity that makes him vividly memorable. The Narrator meets Legrandin casually on the way home from Mass in Combray, but the encounter evokes an image as riveting as an anonymous newspaper photograph that, although seen by chance, long continues to haunt us beyond any possible relevance to our lives:

❝ ... *Tall and handsome of bearing, with a fine, thoughtful face, drooping fair moustaches, blue eyes, an air of disenchantment, an almost exaggerated refinement of courtesy, a talker such as we had never heard, he was in the sight of my family, who never ceased to quote him as an example, the very pattern of a gentleman, who took life in the noblest and most delicate manner. My grandmother alone found fault with him for speaking a little too well, a little too much like a book, for not using a vocabulary as natural as his loosely knotted Lavallière neckties, his short, straight, almost schoolboyish coat. She was astonished, too, at the furious tirades which he was always launching at the aristocracy, at fashionable life, at snobbishness—* "undoubtedly," *he would say,* "the sin of which St Paul is thinking when he speaks of the unforgivable sin against the Holy Ghost".* ❞ [22]

The portrait of Legrandin is no "high-toned shadow," to use a phrase from Henry James. Rather, it bodies forth a veracity that on another level the Nadar portraits also convey. Even though Proust's novel is a supreme creation of the human imagination and a self-contained work of art requiring no verification from the real Paris, Combray, or Balbec, or the genealogy of Boni de Castellane, it conforms to what we believe to have been the real and palpable life of these places and characters.

Having made so much of taking to his bed to complete his life's work, Proust allows us to forget how extraordinary his range of social experience actually was. The power to convey an air of truth, by demonstrating a complete identification with contemporary life, was of course an important part of the nineteenth-century novelist's equipment. When we consider the portly Princesse Mathilde, Napoleon's niece, together with the servants, footmen, and chauffeurs who were also part of the Proustian laboratory, we can begin to comprehend the breadth and richness of the raw material that went into *Remembrance of Things Past*.

When he needed details unavailable to him from his own immediate sources, Proust would take every opportunity to fill in the gaps by close examination of people who just happened to cross his path. Young Harold Nicolson, while a member of the English peace delegation in Paris, encountered the novelist's methods of research the very first time he met Proust. Required to describe every inconsequential detail of his routines in the Foreign Office, Nicolson replied that the staff "generally meet at ten in the morning." Proust interrupted the diplomat insisting that he be more concrete: "No, you're going too fast, begin again. You take the official motor-car, you get out at the Quai d'Orsay, you climb the stairs, you enter the committee room. What happens next?"[23]

If friends or chance acquaintances were not equipped by background or experience to supply him with relevant facts, Proust would hire an "expert" to answer his questions, as in the case of Albert Le Cuziat, a former footman in aristocratic Parisian houses. Aware that Le Cuziat commanded a vast knowledge of genealogy and etiquette, Proust interrogated him mercilessly on all kinds of issues affecting the hypothetical social situations that he planned to incorporate into the novel. Proust called Le Cuziat his "walking Almanach de Gotha," and evening after evening Odilon Albaret the chauffeur would bring the former servant to 102 Boulevard Haussmann to answer such arcane questions as the precedence and seating that should obtain at a dinner party given by the Duchesse de Guermantes.

The number of characters that are drawn from the aristocratic circles Proust knew and admired is not surprising. After all, one of the main themes of the novel is the eventual initiation of the bourgeoisie, with all their ridiculous pretensions, into the vital mysteries and ceremonies of what appeared to be an otherwise exhausted aristocracy. The center of the patrician world represented by the Guermantes family was the upper crust of the Faubourg Saint-Germain. In the novel, the three main events which take place there are the afternoon at Mme de Villeparisis's, the dinner given by the Duchesse de Guermantes, and the soirée of the Princesse de Guermantes. The Faubourg, with its grand eighteenth-century *hôtels*, was the Left Bank district where members of the old nobility had settled after the Restoration, when life at court was no longer possible and the Marais, a still nobler quarter, remained too haunted by memories of those lost during the Revolution. By the time Proust arrived in the Faubourg, it had come to symbolize aristocratic society in all its sacrosanct rituals of existence. The very sound of the residents' names—La Rochefoucauld, Montesquiou, Breteuil, Gramont, Castellane, La Trémoïlle— seemed radiant with magic and mystique, which Proust would later analyze for their historic meaning as he followed the Guermantes Way. When Charlus, greeting guests at the Princesse de Guermantes's, calls out, "Good evening, Mme de La Trémoïlle," it is for Marcel Proust as if a thousand years of French history were echoing in the Baron's salutation.

Having not been born to that class, Proust tirelessly studied even the most trivial matters in the hope of understanding the all but impenetrable milieu represented by the Faubourg Saint-Germain. Certainly, a former footman to a ducal household could be an essential source of information on the inner workings (including the vices) of a closed society at a level that Proust considered crucial. Little wonder, then, that the novelist became obsessed with the private lives of servants, a disclosure made by the rather shocked Duchesse de Clermont-Tonnerre in her memoirs: "And finally we cannot suppress the fact that Proust became enraptured with the study of domestic servants—whether it would be that an element which he encountered nowhere else intrigued his investigative faculties or that he envied servants their greater opportunities for observing the intimate details of things that aroused his interest. In any case, domestic servants in their various embodiments and types were his passion."[24]

In the character of Françoise, the faithful family cook, Proust demonstrates his ability to write sympathetically and with as much sensitivity as he would in the case of an august member of the Jockey Club. After Françoise had walked in and discovered Albertine and the Narrator in intimate embrace, the Narrator subsequently describes his surprise and then reflects upon Françoise's special intelligence:

❝ . . . *Perhaps Françoise had chosen this moment to confound us, having been listening at the door or even peeping through the keyhole. But there was no need to suppose anything of the sort; she might well have scorned to assure herself by the use of her eyes of what her instinct must plainly enough have detected, for by dint of living with me and my parents she had succeeded in acquiring, through fear, prudence, alertness and cunning, that instinctive and almost divinatory knowledge of us all that the mariner has of the sea, the quarry has of the hunter, and if not the physician, often at any rate the invalid has of disease. The amount of knowledge that she managed to acquire would have astounded a stranger with as good reason as does the advanced state of certain arts and sciences among the ancients, given the almost non-existent means of information at their disposal (hers were no less exiguous; they consisted of a few casual remarks forming barely a twentieth part of our conversation at dinner, caught on the wing by the butler and inaccurately transmitted to the kitchen). . . .*❞[25]

Given the profound originality of *Remembrance of Things Past*—an "unconstructable synthesis," in Walter Benjamin's words, of fiction, autobiography, and commentary—a novelist like Proust, who was risking everything in one grand statement, had some legitimate curiosity in all kinds of ingredients. Among them were Nadar's clients, who one by one took their place in front of the camera, unaware that their complexions, tics, clothes, and gestures, their lusts and their pasts would be transformed from one kind of art into another. In *Remembrance of Things Past* Proust time and again evoked the optical mechanics of the camera itself and the vocabulary of photography as the means to recollect the visual reality of more personalities than would ever be assembled in a single piece of fiction, either before or since.

During that famous scene in the Combray church when the Duchesse de Guermantes makes her first appearance, the Narrator imagines himself as a kind of camera set up to record not only the subject's appearance but also her moral self as he sat in the congregation like a voyeur transfixed by the lady's beauty. His eyes become the camera's lens, while his mind serves as both the negative and the print, its image developed by the alchemy of memory combined with some inexplicable reaction to a scene, a sound, a smell, or some physical object acting as the mysterious transforming agent.

But here the simile breaks down because we know how Proust's mind and memory were able to reshape the most ordinary reality into poetic truth. In Proust, the memory, as Howard Moss points out, intervenes at the moment of recording the image between "the enchantments of the past" and the inevitable "disenchantments of the future," thus disrupting the vagaries of chronological time so that time itself is regained as art: "I kept my eyes fixed on her, as though gazing at her I should be able to carry away and store up inside myself the meaning of that prominent nose, those red cheeks and all those details which struck me as so many precious, authentic and singular items of information with regard to her face. . . ."[26]

When Proust's friend the Marquise de Brantes sent him her photograph, the novelist reminded her that his own "imagination" would retouch it "to the point of perfect resemblance," a technique of creation that has never been surpassed in literature.

Swann's Way

Marcel Proust (left) with his mother and brother in 1891.

Mme Adrien Proust (1834—1905)

Jeanne Weil, the daughter of a wealthy Jewish stockbroker, was twenty-one when she married the distinguished Dr. Adrien Proust, then thirty-six years old. Mme Proust was close to her own mother, whose gentle, quiet ways and cultivated love of music and literature she had inherited. Marcel remembered how the two women visited for hours together on art and literature, all the while exchanging quotations from Mme de Sévigné. Later Mme Proust would quote the Marquise in playful reproach to her son for some minor misconduct. Although Proust's mother kept her Jewish faith out of family tradition, Marcel himself was christened at the Church of Saint-Louis d'Antin not long after his birth. Even so, the christening was delayed because of the infant's precarious health. The mature Proust attributed his fragile beginning to the privations and sufferings his mother had endured during the Prussian siege and the Commune that followed.

Proust told his housekeeper, Céleste Albaret, that Mme Proust had often said to him: " 'My poor little Marcel, where would you be without me?' or 'My poor little pet. . . .' Do you know what her last words to me were? 'My poor little canary, what will you do without me? But whatever you do remain a Catholic.' "[1]

To the end of her life in 1905, Jeanne Weil Proust was a protective and indulgent mother, unfailingly sympathetic toward the increasingly eccentric ways of her son, who remained under the same roof with his parents until they died. In fact, the writer's habits of coming and going, of working through the night and sleeping in the day eventually required that mother and son occasionally communicate by letter, even within their own apartment and from room to room. The neurotic, often excessive sentimentality of this correspondence recalls Mme de Sévigné's letters to her daughter, "her most adored object," which also had been frequently dispatched from behind closed doors within the same house. When Dr. Proust complained that his wife was spoiling Marcel, and insisted that the young man must enter some sort of profession, Mme Proust, her son later told Céleste, would "let it all flow over her. I can still hear her saying to father in her gentle voice, 'Have patience, my little doctor. Everything will turn out all right.' "[2]

When Mme Proust died, the distraught thirty-four-year-old Marcel retreated into his bedroom, where he remained throughout a sleepless month, trying to bring his tears under control. The servants, trained by Mme Proust to tiptoe about whenever Marcel was working or sleeping, continued their ingrained, noiseless ways, which finally horrified the novelist by reminding him of his mother.

Just before the end, after considerable suffering had left its mark, Mme Proust begged a friend to photograph her, thereby overcoming the conflict between her desire to leave a last image and her awareness that feigned eagerness and theatrical indifference to an obvious condition could not prevent the picture from being an unbearably sad one. Proust would later transfer the episode to the Narrator's grandmother, who asks Saint-Loup to take her photograph:

❝Unfortunately, the displeasure that was aroused in me by the prospect of this photographic session, and more particularly by the delight with which my grandmother appeared to be looking forward to it, was sufficiently apparent for Françoise to notice it and to do her best, unintentionally, to increase it by making me a sentimental, gushing speech by which I refused to appear moved.

"Oh, Monsieur, my poor Madame will be so pleased at having her likeness taken. She's going to wear the hat that her old Françoise has trimmed for her: you must let her."

I persuaded myself that it was not cruel of me to mock Françoise's sensibility, by reminding myself that my mother and grandmother, my models in all things, often did the same. But my grandmother, noticing that I seemed put out, said that if her sitting for her photograph offended me in any way she would give up the idea. I would not hear of it. I assured her that I saw no harm in it, and let her adorn herself, but, thinking to show how shrewd and forceful I was, added a few sarcastic and wounding words calculated to neutralise the pleasure which she seemed to find in being photographed, with the result that, if I was obliged to see my grandmother's magnificent hat, I succeeded at least in driving from her face that joyful expression which ought to have made me happy. Alas, it too often happens, while the people we love best are still alive, that such expressions appear to us as the exasperating manifestation of some petty whim rather than as the precious form of the happiness which we should dearly like to procure for them. My ill-humour arose more particularly from the fact that, during that week, my grandmother had appeared to be avoiding me, and I had not been able to have her to myself for a moment, either by night or day. When I came back in the afternoon to be alone with her for a little I was told that she was not in the hotel; or else she would shut herself up with Françoise for endless confabulations which I was not permitted to interrupt. And when, after being out all evening with Saint-Loup, I had been thinking on the way home of the moment at which I should be able to go to my grandmother and embrace her, I waited in vain for her to give the three little knocks on the party wall which would tell me to go in and say good night to her. At length I would go to bed, a little resentful of her for depriving me, with an indifference so new and strange in her, of a joy on which I had counted so much, and I would lie there for a while, my heart throbbing as in my childhood, listening to the wall which remained silent, until I cried myself to sleep. 』³

Like the withheld taps on the wall, the additional goodnight kiss refused by the Narrator's mother has set off some of the most celebrated psychological and critical speculations in the history of modern literature. The meaning of the omitted gesture, its creative implications as well as its painful psychic impact, has at times threatened to overwhelm the general perception of Proust, his life, and the complex roots of his achievements.

In the life of both Proust and his Narrator, the importance of a mother's indulgence cannot be exaggerated. The Narrator's recollection of his convulsive sobs—when as a child he was finally confronted by his mother's decision, made as a consequence of his own manipulations, to spend the night in his room—often echoes, sometimes at the scarcely audible level of an inner voice, the Narrator's emotional meditations throughout the novel:

❝My mother opened the latticed door which led from the hall to the staircase. Presently I heard her coming upstairs to close her window. I went quietly into the passage; my heart was beating so violently that I could hardly move, but at least it was throbbing no longer with anxiety, but with terror and joy. I saw in the well of the stair a light coming upwards, from Mamma's candle. Then I saw Mamma herself and I threw myself upon her. For an instant she looked at me in astonishment, not realising what could have happened. Then her face assumed an expression of anger. She said not a single word to me; and indeed I used to go for days on end without being spoken to, for far more venial offenses than this. A single word from Mamma would have been an admission *that further intercourse with me was within the bounds of possibility, and that might perhaps have appeared to me more terrible still, as indicating that, with such a punishment as was in store for me, mere silence and black looks would have been puerile.* "[4]

After his mother finally submitted to this blackmail, doing so with the encouragement of her husband to "go along with the child," the Narrator never succeeds in letting his father know the gratitude he feels toward him for this kindness:

" *... Many years have passed since that night. The wall of the staircase up which I had watched the light of his candle gradually climb was long ago demolished. And in myself, too, many things have perished which I imagined would last for ever, and new ones have risen, giving birth to new sorrows and new joys which in those days I could not have foreseen, just as now the old are hard to understand. It is a long time, too, since my father has been able to say to Mamma: "Go along with the child." Never again will such moments be possible for me. But of late I have been increasingly able to catch, if I listen attentively, the sound of the sobs which I had the strength to control in my father's presence, and which broke out only when I found myself alone with Mamma. In reality their echo has never ceased; and it is only because life is now growing more and more quiet round about me that I hear them anew, like those convent bells which are so effectively drowned during the day by the noises of the street that one would suppose them to have stopped, until they ring out again through the silent evening air.* "[5]

Robert Proust (1873–1935)

Céleste Albaret, the novelist's devoted housekeeper, revealed a remarkably accurate instinct in the observations she recorded about the Proust family. "Whatever they had in common," she wrote of Marcel and his brother Robert, they "inherited from their father," and this "was an indefatigable capacity to concentrate and work. They merely chose different fields."[1]

Like his father, Robert Proust became a distinguished physician, a member of the Faculty of Medicine at the University of Paris, and would be invested with the Legion of Honor. Science and medicine were life to Robert Proust, and his admiring brother wrote that, just as their father had done, Robert "put his heart and soul into his career."[2]

The birth of Robert when Marcel was two years old produced in the sensitive older brother a not surprising jealousy and filial anxiety, which made their lifelong relationship more formal than intimate. A sense of family duty and their respective obsessions with work allowed the two Proust men to maintain loyal, if perfunctory, ties to one another.

Robert, with his easygoing, healthy, well-ordered ways, must have found his neurotic, unpredictable brother something of a trial, on more than one occasion. A particularly difficult moment came at his wedding on a cold February day in 1903. Marcel, the best man, arrived at the church swathed in mufflers and protected by three coats worn

over his white tie and tails. The resulting bulk prevented Proust from passing along the pews to collect the traditional offering, and so he stood in the aisle, "his Lazarus-like face with its melancholy mustache rising like a surprise out of his woolly black cerements. He felt he had to explain himself, and to each row in turn he announced in a loud voice that he was not able to dress otherwise, that he had been ill for months, that he would be still more ill that evening, that it was not his fault."[3] He followed his announcement with a return to his bed, straight from the reception, and remained there for another several weeks.

After attempting, in an early draft of the novel, to write a trivial scene involving his brother, where Robert's only line is "Marcel has had more chocolate blancmange than me!" Proust dropped the character altogether in the final version.

Mme Émile Straus (1845–1926)
Duchesse de Guermantes, Odette

Geneviève Bizet-Straus had been briefly and happily married to the composer Georges Bizet when he died in 1875. Proust and her son Jacques Bizet were classmates at the Cours Pape-Carpentier, a preparatory school. The beautiful sympathetic widow may have accompanied the two boys on their daily walk to school. Seven years later, Proust, her precocious admirer, would be introduced into the Straus salon, after which he remained the hostess's friend for the rest of his life.

The ascent of Mme Straus into society and the establishment of her celebrated salon in the Rue de Douai came rather quickly after she married the attorney Émile Straus (said by some to be the illegitimate half-brother of Barons Alphonse, Gustave, and Edmond de Rothschild). Considered a beauty in her day, Mme Straus achieved an elegance of dress, not to mention the setting of her drawing room, that gave this Proustian heroine a special renown throughout Parisian society. But it was her wit that Proust chose to immortalize in the Guermantes family and in the person of the Duchess.

At the age of twenty Proust revealed his infatuation when he wrote a letter and headed it "The Truth about Madame Straus":

At first I believed you loved only beautiful things and that you understood them well— and then I saw that you didn't give a hang about them; then I thought you liked people, and now I see that you don't give a hang about them either. I only believe you love a certain kind of life which brings out your intelligence less than your wit, your wit less than your tact, your tact less than your clothes. A person who more than anything loves this kind of life—and who, nevertheless, casts a spell! And it is just because you are enchanting that you must not rejoice and decide that I love you less. [1]

That "certain kind of life" created by Mme Straus, a life which brought out her special intelligence, cast its spell over a number of great admirers, among them Forain, Degas, and Gaston Calmette, the editor of *Le Figaro*. Open and socially liberal, the Straus salon was marked by its enlightened, spirited concern for contemporary political issues. Although its hostess may not have worn black, as rumor had it, the day Dreyfus was condemned, her salon did become the headquarters of the Dreyfusards, and it was there that Jacques Bizet, her Halévy nephews, and Proust organized the first *Aurore* petition.

As each section of *Rememberance of Things Past* appeared, Proust rushed a copy to his ancient friend, now confined to a solitary life in darkened rooms. And volume by volume of the "daring and magnificent book" would restore Mme Straus at least momentarily, reminding her of all the evenings when the young and admiring Proust came and discussed every conceivable subject with his unshockable friend. The physical and intellectual revival that she experienced when the eagerly awaited copy arrived is touchingly revealed in one of her last letters to the novelist, written on May 13, 1922:

I take the book, I cut the pages and say to myself: I shall read for a quarter of an hour; and then the quarter hour goes by. . . . I read. . . . I continue to read. Dinner is announced. I say: "I am coming," . . . and I go on reading. The servant returns timidly

and does not leave—so, embarrassed by her perjorative presence, I go downstairs. After dinner we come back up, and very quietly, as though I were doing nothing, I discreetly draw out the precious book . . . and then I am plunged back into reading, until the impetuous lawyer, whom you know so well, cries out with a vehemence of which you are also not unaware: "But this is abominable, this woman who reads all the time, morning, noon, and night she reads, she reads, she reads, all the time."

This little picture of my life in the last two days will express more than all the compliments in the world and will explain the reason why I haven't thanked you sooner for having sent me these three last rare copies of Sodome et Gomorrhe.[2]

Charles Haas (1832–1901)
Swann

The lacquered surface of a Noh mask reveals as much personality as Nadar's portrait of Charles Haas. The sleek, peregrine quality of the face, with its quizzical, slightly raised eyebrows and the upturned mustache left over from the Second Empire, implies a certain aloofness, challenging us to find a single clue to the character or the origins of the man hidden behind the mask. Proust actually was more like an acquaintance than an intimate, even though he chose Haas to be the exemplar of his novel's hero. Yet there was an elusive social perfection and reserve about Haas that no doubt captured Proust's imagination as a stimulating role model for his idealized character.

By the time Proust first observed him, Haas, like Swann, "had so long ceased to direct his life towards any ideal goal, confining himself to the ephemeral satisfactions, that he had come to believe, without ever admitting it to himself in so many words, that he would remain in that condition for the rest of his days."[1]

Also like Swann, Haas was a masterful social climber, performing feats of breathtaking skill as he maneuvered his way up the glacial slopes of Parisian society. As a connoisseur of the type, Proust admired Haas's self-confident control and, once expressed in Swann, the "grace of movement of a trained gymnast whose supple limbs will carry out precisely what is required without any clumsy participation by the rest of his body." Moreover, "the simple and elementary gestures of a man of the world as he courteously holds out his hand to the unknown youth who is introduced to him, or bows discreetly to the ambassador to whom he is introduced, had gradually pervaded the whole of Swann's social deportment without his being conscious of it."[2]

Funerals in Paris were like those celebrated occasions in Boston when one's appearance among the mourners measured the height of one's social standing. A brief report, published in *Le Gaulois*, of the funeral held for the Comtesse de Ludre provides as good a source as any for determining Haas's precise rank among the leading gentlemen of his time:

The funeral of the Comtesse de Ludre, née Beauveau, took place yesterday at ten o'clock in the Church of Saint-Honoré d'Eyleau. The Ducs de Montmorency, Bisaccia, d'Estissac, de Noailles, de Blacas, de Clermont-Tonnerre, de Mouchy, Prince Murat, Prince de Poix, Marquis de Breteuil, Baron Adolphe de Rothschild, Comtesse Paul de Pourtalès, Comte de Noailles, Comte Charles de Breteuil, Marquis du Lau, Comte Aimery de La Rochefoucauld, M. Lavedan, M. Charles Haas.

Haas may have been at the end of this roll call of the period's great names, but the fact that the son of a nineteenth-century Jewish stockbroker would have any place whatever in such illustrious company signified the sort of achievement the young Marcel Proust admired and no doubt envied.

Mme Straus immediately dubbed him Swann-Haas when the novel began to appear, even though Proust denied, at least at first, that the well-bred, enigmatic Haas was at all related to his fictional character.

In the "Overture," we find Swann introduced by the Narrator at the very outset of the novel. He is the first major character, other than those of the Narrator's own family, to enter the story, the occasion provided by the Narrator's recollection of his visits to Combray, the village where his grandparents and great-aunt lived:

For many years, during the course of which—especially before his marriage—M. Swann the younger came often to see them at Combray, my great-aunt and my grandparents never suspected that he had entirely ceased to live in the society which his family had frequented, and that, under the sort of incognito which the name of Swann gave him among us, they were harbouring—with the complete innocence of a family of respectable innkeepers who have in their midst some celebrated highwayman without knowing it—one of the most distinguished members of the Jockey Club, a particular friend of the Comte de Paris and of the Prince of Wales, and one of the men most sought after in the aristocratic world of the Faubourg Saint-Germain.

Our utter ignorance of the brilliant social life which Swann led was, of course, due in part to his own reserve and discretion, but also to the fact that middle-class people in those days took what was almost a Hindu view of society, which they held to consist of sharply defined castes, so that everyone at his birth found himself called to that station in life which his parents already occupied, and from which nothing, save the accident of an exceptional career or of a "good" marriage, could extract you and translate you to a superior caste. M. Swann the elder had been a stockbroker; and so "young Swann" found himself immured for life in a caste whose members' fortunes, as in a category of tax-payers, varied between such and such limits of income. One knew the people with whom his father had associated, and so one knew his own associates, the people with whom he was "in a position to mix."...

But if anyone had suggested to my great-aunt that this Swann, who, in his capacity as the son of old M. Swann, was "fully qualified" to be received by any of the "best people," by the most respected barristers and solicitors of Paris (though he was perhaps a trifle inclined to let this hereditary privilege go by default), had another almost secret existence of a wholly different kind; that when he left our house in Paris, saying that he must go home to bed, he would no sooner have turned the corner than he would stop, retrace his steps, and be off to some salon on whose like no stockbroker or associate of stockbrokers had ever set eyes—that would have seemed to my aunt as extraordinary ... as the thought of having had to dinner Ali Baba, who, as soon as he finds himself alone and unobserved, will make his way into the cave, resplendent with its unsuspected treasures.

Gabriel Hanotaux (1853–1944)
Norpois

A friend of Proust's father, Dr. Adrien Proust, Gabriel Hanotaux was named Minister of Foreign Affairs in 1894. He later served as France's Ambassador to Rome. It was through Hanotaux that Proust managed to have himself recommended for a post in the Mazarine Library in 1895. Since it required no more than ten to twenty hours a week, the unpaid assistantship promised to be a respectable position for an aspiring young writer with independent means. In the end, however, the job proved too much for the incumbent's delicate constitution. Proust emerged from the library dust each day armed with a throat spray, which he used as soon as he was outside. The Mazarine appointment lasted only a few months.

Hanotaux was Foreign Minister when Emperor Nicholas II of Russia, called Theodosius II in *Remembrance of Things Past*, made a state visit to the French capital. As if to rehearse the role of M. de Norpois, Hanotaux attended the official dinner and then related the details of the occasion to the Proust family. Moreover, it was Norpois in *Within a Budding Grove* who gave the Narrator his first literary encouragement. Also like Hanotaux, Norpois combined writing with his diplomatic career, by grinding out tiresome histories and newspaper articles on public affairs:

❛*I was introduced to him before dinner by my father, who summoned me into his study for the purpose. As I entered, the Ambassador rose, held out his hand, bowed his tall figure and fixed his blue eyes attentively on my face. As the foreign visitors who used to be presented to him, in the days when he still represented France abroad, were all more or less (even the famous singers) persons of note, with regard to whom he therefore knew that he would be able to say later on, when he heard their names mentioned in Paris or in Petersburg, that he remembered perfectly the evening he had spent with them in Munich or Sofia, he had formed the habit of impressing upon them, by his affability, the pleasure he felt in making their acquaintance; but in addition to this, being convinced that in the life of foreign capitals, in contact at once with all the interesting personalities that passed through them and with the manners and customs of the native populations, one acquired a deeper insight than could be gleaned from books into the history, the geography, the traditions of the different nations, and into the intellectual trends of Europe, he would exercise upon each newcomer his keen power of observation, so as to decide at once with what manner of man he had to deal. It was some time since the Government had entrusted him with a post abroad, but as soon as anyone was introduced to him, his eyes, as though they had not yet received notification of their master's retirement, began their fruitful observation, while by his whole attitude he endeavoured to convey that the stranger's name was not unknown to him. And so, while speaking to me kindly and with the air of self-importance of a man who is conscious of the vastness of his experience, he never ceased to examine me with a sagacious curiosity for his own profit, as though I had been some exotic custom, some historic and instructive monument or some star on tour. And in this way he gave proof, in his attitude towards me, at once of the majestic benevolence of the sage Mentor and of the zealous curiosity of the young Anacharsis. . . .*

    "A friend of mine has a son whose case, mutatis mutandis, is very much like yours." He adopted in speaking of our common prediposition the same reassuring tone as if it had been a predisposition not for literature but for rheumatism, and he had wished to assure me that it would not necessarily prove fatal. "He too chose to leave the Quai d'Orsay, although the way had been paved for him there by his father, and without caring what people might say, he settled down to write. And certainly, he's had no reason to regret it. He published two years ago—of course, he's much older than you— a book about the Sense of the Infinite on the western shore of Lake Victoria Nyanza, and this year he has brought out a short treatise, less weighty but written with a lively, not to say cutting pen, on the Repeating Rifle in the Bulgarian Army; and these have put him quite in a class by himself. He's already gone pretty far, and he's not the sort of man to stop half way. I happen to know that (without any suggestion, of course, of his standing for election) his name has been mentioned several times in conversation, and not at all unfavourably, at the Academy of Moral Sciences. And so, though one can't say yet, of course, that he's exactly at the pinnacle, he has fought his way by sheer merit to a very fine position indeed, and success—which doesn't always come only to the pushers and the muddlers, the mountebanks and the humbugs—success has crowned his efforts".❜[1]

Mme Aubernon de Nerville
(1825–1899)
Mme Verdurin

Lydie Aubernon, who figures in the fictional portrait of Mme Verdurin, began her career as a hostess under the supervision of her mother, whose own drawing room had been famous in the reign of Louis-Philippe. After her mother died, Mme Aubernon confessed to Edmond de Goncourt: "I miss her often, but only a little at a time."[1] Proust would later have Swann *père* make the same remark on the death of his wife.

Fat, lively, vulgar, the sixty-seven-year-old Mme Aubernon said she knew her looks had gone once men offered compliments only on her intelligence. Before her weekly Saturday reception Mme Aubernon always gave dinner to twelve invited guests whom she had informed of the topic to be discussed that evening. Mme Straus, when asked her opinion on adultery, the announced subject for that occasion, excused herself saying she had prepared on incest by mistake. During the Dreyfus affair, a rival hostess inquired of Mme Aubernon what she was doing with her Jews. Coolly, she replied: "I'm keeping them on."[2]

Mme Aubernon's drawing room was famous for its theatricals, and it was there that Ibsen's *A Doll's House* and *John Gabriel Borkman* had their first performances in France. Buried in a book of Ibsen's one day, the *saloniste* told a visitor not to disturb her as she was busy acquiring "a Norwegian soul"![3]

Dr. Samuel Pozzi (1846–1918)
Cottard

A surgeon with a practice drawn from the ranks of the *haute bourgeoisie*, Pozzi was also a member of the Academy of Medicine and a Senator from the Dordogne. The fifteen-year-old Marcel met Dr. Pozzi when he came to dine with the Prousts. Although admitted to the salon of Princesse Mathilde, Pozzi struck Léon Daudet as "talkative, hollow, and reeking of hair oil." Daudet claimed he would not have trusted the surgeon even to perform the services of a barber, "especially if there had been a mirror in the room."[1]

Dr. Pozzi's infidelities—to his wife the physician claimed his deceptions only supplemented her—provided, as did his vanities, prototypes of behavior for Dr. Cottard in *Swann's Way*. Also modeled on Victor Blancard, Dr. Cottard figures in Mme Verdurin's "little clan":

❝Dr. Cottard was never quite certain of the tone in which he ought to reply to any observation, or whether the speaker was jesting or in earnest. And so by way of precaution he would embellish all his facial expressions with the offer of a conditional, a provisional smile whose expectant subtlety would exonerate him from the charge of being a simpleton, if the remark addressed to him should turn out to have been facetious. But as he must also be prepared to face the alternative, he dared not allow this smile to assert itself positively on his features, and you would see there a perpetually flickering uncertainty, in which could be deciphered the question that he never dared to ask: "Do you really mean that?" He was no more confident of the manner in which he ought to conduct himself in the street, or indeed in life generally, than he was in a drawing-room; and he might be seen greeting passers-by, carriages, and anything that occurred with a knowing smile which absolved his subsequent behaviour of all impropriety, since it proved, if it should turn out unsuited to the occasion, that he was well aware of that, and that if he had assumed a smile, the jest was a secret of his own.❞[2]

Professor Georges Dieulafoy
(1839–1911)

At the Hôtel-Dieu, Paris' municipal hospital, Dr. Dieulafoy had occupied the chair of internal medicine until 1896, when he was made Professor. With his "exaggerated good looks" and his "decorum suited to distressing circumstances," the physician plays himself in *The Guermantes Way*, as the doctor asked to certify the death of Marcel's grandmother:

❝At this point my father hurried from the room. I supposed that a sudden change, for better or worse, had occurred. It was simply that Dr. Dieulafoy had just arrived. My father went to receive him in the drawing-room, like the actor who is next to appear on the stage. He had been sent for not to cure but to certify, almost in a legal capacity. Dr. Dieulafoy may indeed have been a great physician, a marvellous teacher; to the several roles in which he excelled, he added another, in which he remained for forty years without a rival, a role as original as that of the confidant, the clown or the noble father, which consisted in coming to certify that a patient was in extremis. His name alone presaged the dignity with which he would sustain the part, and when the servant announced: "M. Dieulafoy," one thought one was in a Molière play. To the dignity of his bearing was added, without being conspicuous, the litheness of a perfect figure. His exaggerated good looks were tempered by a decorum suited to distressing circumstances. In the sable majesty of his frock coat the Professor would enter the room, melancholy without affectation, uttering not one word of condolence that could have been construed as insincere, nor being guilty of the slightest infringement of the rules of tact. At the foot of a deathbed it was he and not the Duc de Guermantes who was the great nobleman. Having examined my grandmother without tiring her, and with an excess of reserve which was an act of courtesy to the doctor in charge of the case, he murmured a few words to my father, and bowed respectfully to my mother, to whom I felt that my father had positively to restrain himself from saying: "Professor Dieulafoy." But already the latter had turned away, not wishing to seem intrusive, and made a perfect exit, simply accepting the sealed envelope that was slipped into his hand. He did not appear to have seen it, and we ourselves were left wondering for a moment whether we had really given it to him, with such a conjurer's dexterity had he made it vanish without sacrificing one iota of the gravity—which was if anything accentuated—of the eminent consultant in his long frock coat with its silk lapels, his noble features engraved with the most dignified commiseration. His deliberation and his vivacity combined to show that, even if he had a hundred other calls to make, he did not wish to appear to be in a hurry. For he was the embodiment of tact, intelligence and kindness. The eminent man is no longer with us. Other physicians, other professors, may have rivalled, may indeed have surpassed him. But the "capacity" in which his knowledge, his physical endowments, his distinguished manners made him supreme exists no longer, for want of any successor capable of taking his place. Mamma had not even noticed M. Dieulafoy: everything that was not my grandmother no longer existed. I remember (and here I anticipate) that at the cemetery, where we saw her, like a supernatural apparition, tremulously approach the grave, her eyes seeming to gaze after a being that had taken wing and was already far away, . . .❞[1]

Madeleine Lemaire (1845–1928)
Mme Verdurin

Zestful *saloniste* immortalized in the novel for her contribution to the personality of Mme Verdurin, Madeleine maintained one of the period's most brilliant salons at her house in the Rue de Monceau. The author of greatly admired paintings of roses, Mme Lemaire would often receive guests while seated in front of her easel in the salon. It was in 1892 that Proust first entered her crowded, suffocating rooms, where artists, poets, playwrights, Duchesses, Countesses, and their companions overflowed into the garden and a glass-roofed studio annex.

Tall, handsome, and driven by bourgeois energy, Mme Lemaire reveals even in Nadar's formal portrait a casual, open blowsiness beneath her evening gown, suggesting the informality that delighted her guests from all ranks of society. Word of her hospitality, especially to musicians, spread rapidly, and it soon brought carriages from the Faubourg Saint-Germain crowding into the Monceau streets on Tuesdays during the regular season that Mme Lemaire held from April to June:

Mme Verdurin sat alone, the twin hemispheres of her pale, slightly roseate brow magnificently bulging, her hair drawn back, partly in imitation of an eighteenth-century portrait, partly from the need for coolness of a feverish person reluctant to reveal her condition, aloof, a deity presiding over the musical rites, goddess of Wagnerism and sick-headaches, a sort of almost tragic Norn, conjured up by the spell of genius in the midst of all these "bores," in whose presence she would scorn even more than usual to express her feelings upon hearing a piece of music which she knew better than they. . . .

I looked at the Mistress, whose fierce immobility seemed to be a protest against the rhythmic noddings of the ignorant heads of the ladies of the Faubourg. She did not say: "You realise, of course, that I know a thing or two about this music! If I were to express all that I feel, you'd never hear the end of it!" She did not say this. But her upright, motionless body, her expressionless eyes, her straying locks said it for her. They spoke also of her courage, said that the musicians could carry on, that they need not spare her nerves, that she would not flinch at the andante, would not cry out at the allegro. . . .[1]

The Verdurins never invited you to dinner; you had your "place laid" there. There was never any programme for the evening's entertainment. The young pianist would play, but only if "the spirit moved him," for no one was forced to do anything, and, as M. Verdurin used to say: "We're all friends here. Liberty Hall, you know!"

If the pianist suggested playing the Ride of the Valkyries or the Prelude to Tristan, Mme Verdurin would protest, not because the music was displeasing to her, but, on the contrary, because it made too violent an impression on her. "Then you want me to have one of my headaches? You know quite well it's the same every time he plays that. I know what I'm in for. To-morrow, when I want to get up—nothing doing!" If he was not going to play they talked, and one of the friends—usually the painter who was in favour there that year—would "spin," as M. Verdurin put it, "a damned funny yarn that made 'em all split with laughter," and especially Mme Verdurin, who had such an inveterate habit of taking literally the figurative descriptions of her emotions that Dr. Cottard (then

a promising young practitioner) had once had to reset her jaw, which she had dislocated from laughing too much.

Evening dress was barred, because you were all "good pals" and didn't want to look like the "boring people" who were to be avoided like the plague and only asked to the big evenings, which were given as seldom as possible and then only if it would amuse the painter or make the musician better known. . . . "[2]

Camille Barrère (1851–1940)
Norpois

arrère, an old family friend and a political colleague of Dr. Proust in his efforts to rid Europe of cholera, identified himself as Norpois when *Within a Budding Grove* appeared in 1919. A distinguished diplomat who had served as France's Ambassador to Rome from 1897 to 1924, Barrère failed to be amused by the portrait. Proust said that Barrère made his assumptions about the casting "simply because he used to dine with us every week when I was a child, whereas M. de Norpois was a representative of a diplomatic type which is the exact opposite of M. Barrère though no less utterly detestable."[1] The novelist once wrote his mother that he had seen the enigmatic, mandarin, self-conscious Ambassador pass by the apartment and could assure her that he did "not look like Saint Francis of Assisi,"[2] an apparent reference to the diplomat's recent post at the Quirinale.

Mme Proust too was not very favorably impressed by Barrère, just as the Narrator's mother would disclose her reservations about Norpois:

❛As for my mother, perhaps the Ambassador had not the type of mind towards which she felt herself most attracted. And it must be said that his conversation furnished so exhaustive a glossary of the superannuated forms of speech peculiar to a certain profession, class and period—a period which, for that profession and that class, might be said not to have altogether passed away—that I sometimes regret not having kept a literal record simply of the things that I heard him say.❜[3]

Still, Proust wittily reinvents the Ambassador's "superannuated" rhetoric in the dinner conversation during which the Narrator's father queries the diplomat about his encounter with King Theodosius, recently in France on a state visit:

❛"And I trust you are satisfied with the results of his visit?" "Enchanted! One was justified in feeling some apprehension as to the manner in which a sovereign who is still so young would handle such an awkward situation, particularly at this highly delicate juncture. For my own part, I had complete confidence in the King's political sense. But I must confess that he far surpassed my expectations. The speech that he made at the Elysée, which, according to information that has come to me from a most authoritative source, was composed from beginning to end by the King himself, was fully deserving of the interest that it has aroused in all quarters. It was simply masterly; a trifle daring, I quite admit, but it was an audacity which, after all, was fully justified by the event. Traditional diplomacy is all very well in its way, but in practice it has made his country and ours live in a hermetically sealed atmosphere in which it was no longer possible to breathe. Very well! There is one method of letting in fresh air, obviously not a method that one could officially recommend, but one which King Theodosius could allow himself to adopt—and that is to break the windows. Which he accordingly did, with a spontaneous good humour that delighted everybody, and also with an aptness in his choice of words in which one could at once detect the race of scholarly princes from whom he is descended through his mother. There can be no question that when he spoke of the 'affinities' that bind his country to France, the expression, unusual though it be in the vocabulary of the chancelleries, was a singularly happy one . . . ".❜[4]

Reynaldo Hahn (1875–1947)

Singer, pianist, and composer of promise, Reynaldo Hahn met Proust in 1893, when he was nineteen and the future novelist twenty-two. William Sansom has described Hahn as "pale brown, handsome, gifted, Jewish, moustached."[1] The young man had come to Paris from his native Venezuela to study at the Conservatoire under Massenet and Saint-Saëns. Hahn and Proust were introduced at Madeleine Lemaire's Tuesdays in the Rue de Monceau, where the performance the musician gave of his own setting of Verlaine's *Les Chansons grises* became something of a sensation. Later Hahn would make songs of Proust's four short poems on the painters Cuyp, Potter, Watteau, and van Dyke. He sang them too at Mme Lemaire's, accompanied by a pianist specially imported from Chartres.

The two gifted young men began an intimate and passionate relationship that continued for the next two years, and remained a loyal attachment for the rest of Proust's life. Although no character in *Remembrance of Things Past* can be specifically identified with Hahn, the composer's personality, his friendship with Proust, and his musical taste inspired many details throughout the novel. Hahn was one of the few friends whom Proust allowed to read the opening chapter of *Remembrance of Things Past*, and his favorable reaction encouraged the author to continue with it.

Musically, Hahn adhered to the classical tradition, and he tried to lure Proust away from such innovators as Fauré and Debussy. Although unsuccessful, he did introduce Proust to the music of Saint-Saëns, and, with Hahn, Proust first heard the Saint-Saëns Sonata in D Minor for violin and piano at one of Mme Lemaire's gatherings. Captivated by the principal theme found in the first movement, he later asked Hahn to repeat the haunting melody for him: "Play me that bit I like, Reynaldo—you know 'the little phrase.' "[2] It was to become the leitmotif of his love for Hahn, just as the Vinteuil Sonata would become that of Swann's love for Odette:

❝ . . . *He would enter the drawing-room; and there, while Mme Verdurin . . . sent him to the place kept for him beside Odette, the pianist would play to them—for their two selves—the little phrase by Vinteuil which was, so to speak, the national anthem of their love. He began, always, with the sustained tremolos of the violin part which for several bars was heard alone, filling the whole foreground; until suddenly it seemed to draw aside, and—as in those interiors by Pieter de Hooch which are deepened by the narrow frame of a half-opened door, in the far distance, of a different colour, velvety with the radiance of some intervening light—the little phrase appeared, dancing, pastoral, interpolated, episodic, belonging to another world. It rippled past, simple and immortal, scattering on every side the bounties of its grace, with the same ineffable smile . . . he contemplated the little phrase less in its own light—in what it might express to a musician who knew nothing of the existence of him and Odette when he had composed it, and to all those who would hear it in centuries to come—than as a pledge, a token of his love, which made even the Verdurins and their young pianist think of Odette at the same time as himself—which bound her to him by a lasting tie; so much so that (whimsically entreated by Odette) he had abandoned the idea of getting some "professional" to play over to him the whole sonata, of which he still knew no more than this one passage. "Why do you want the rest?" she had asked him. "Our little bit; that's all we need."* . . . ❞[3]

Jeanne Pouquet
Gilberte

Famous as Gilberte, Jeanne Pouquet would be introduced to Proust, six years after this photograph was made, by her fiancé and the novelist's friend Gaston Arman de Caivallet. With her shy beauty, she immediately captivated the young Marcel. There is a well-known photograph of Jeanne with Proust at her feet strumming on a tennis racquet for a guitar. The picture captures not only the spirit of a small band of young *copains* but also the romantic feeling the twenty-year-old Proust had for his friend's beloved, a feeling that went unrequited. Later, Jeanne would become the golden-haired Gilberte of *Remembrance of Things Past*. In 1912, when the early version of the Gilberte idyll was about to appear in *Le Figaro*, Proust wrote to Jeanne: "You will find amalgamated in it something of my feelings when I wasn't sure whether you would be at the tennis court. But what's the use of recalling things which you took the absurd and unkind course of pretending never to notice."[1] Later he confessed to his housekeeper, Céleste Albaret: "I was in love with her as one can never love again."

As with his extravagant courtship of the Comtesse Laure de Chevigné and Mme Straus, the question of Proust's love for and appreciation of women is raised, a question that biographers have attempted to address but without arriving at completely satisfactory answers. It has often been argued, for example by George Painter, that Proust's heterosexual love affairs were genuine, based always, as Freud would hold, on homosexual motives. Pursuing this argument, Painter asserts that Proust's infatuations followed a classic pattern in that they involved women who for reasons of marriage, class, or age were unobtainable, a classic pattern of such doomed affairs. Proust's friend Antoine Bibesco, writing in his memoirs, dismisses all such romantic, sentimental attachments as pure whimsy.

Here, in a passage from *Swann's Way*, is the Narrator's recollection of his first sight of Gilberte:

> *The hedge afforded a glimpse, inside the park, of an alley bordered with jasmine, pansies, and verbenas, among which the stocks held open their fresh plump purses, of a pink as fragrant and as faded as old Spanish leather, while a long green hose, coiling across the gravel, sent up from its sprinkler a vertical and prismatic fan of multicoloured droplets. Suddenly I stood still, unable to move, as happens when we are faced with a vision that appeals not to our eyes only but requires a deeper kind of perception and takes possession of the whole of our being. A little girl with fair, reddish hair, who appeared to be returning from a walk, and held a trowel in her hand, was looking at us, raising towards us a face powdered with pinkish freckles. Her black eyes gleamed, . . .*
>
> *I gazed at her, at first with that gaze which is not merely the messenger of the eyes, but at whose window all the senses assemble and lean out, petrified and anxious, a gaze eager to reach, touch, capture, bear off in triumph the body at which it is aimed, and the soul with the body; then . . . with another, an unconsciously imploring look, whose object was to force her to pay attention to me, to see, to know me. She cast a glance forwards and sideways, so as to take stock of my grandfather and my father, and doubtless the impression she formed was that we were all ridiculous people, for she turned away with an indifferent and disdainful air, and stood sideways so as to spare her face the indignity of remaining within their field of vision; and while they, continuing to walk on without noticing her, overtook and passed me, she went on staring out of the corner of her eye in my*

direction, without any particular expression, without appearing to see me, but with a fixity and a half-hidden smile which I could only interpret, from the notions I had been vouchsafed of good breeding, as a mark of infinite contempt; and her hand, at the same time, sketched in the air an indelicate gesture, for which, when it was addressed in public to a person whom one did not know, the little dictionary of manners which I carried in my mind supplied only one meaning, namely, a deliberate insult.

"Gilberte, come along; what are you doing?" called out in a piercing tone of authority a lady in white whom I had not seen until that moment, . . . Thus was wafted to my ears the name of Gilberte, bestowed on me like a talisman which might, perhaps, enable me some day to rediscover her whom its syllables had just endowed with an identity, whereas the moment before she had been merely an uncertain image. . . . "[2]

Willie Heath

The characteristics that seem most essentially to define the various groups of Proust's friends are intelligence, looks, class, and style. Willie Heath belongs with such handsome, gifted companions as Reynaldo Hahn and Lucien Daudet. Bourgeois rather than young noblemen from the Faubourg, these comrades dominated the affections of Proust during the 1890s as he moved along the Guermantes Way, dreaming of "living in a chosen circle of noble-minded men and women, far from the arrows of stupidity, vice and malice."[1]

English-born and Protestant, Heath had been converted to Catholicism at the age of twelve. His refined, melancholy gaze reminded Marcel of the pensive, doomed English Cavaliers in van Dyck's portraits hanging in the Louvre. "Their elegance, like yours," Proust later wrote of Willie, "lies not so much in their clothes as in their bodies, and their bodies seem to have received it, and to continue unceasingly to receive it, from their souls; for it is a moral elegance."[2]

Their friendship was cut short when Heath succumbed to typhoid fever on October 3, 1893, little more than three months after Nadar had photographed him in June of that year. In 1894 Proust dedicated *Les Plaisirs et les jours* to the dead Englishman, recalling their encounter in the Bois, where the early light falling on Heath's countenance and his finger pointed toward Heaven suggested something of Leonardo's *Saint John the Baptist*:

"Souvent le doigt levé, les yeux impénétrables et souriants en face de l'enigme que vous taisiez, vous m'êtes apparu comme le Saint-Jean Baptiste de Léonard. Nous formions alors le rêve, presque le projet de vivre de plus en plus l'un avec l'autre, dans un cercle de femmes et d'hommes magnanimes et choisis, assez loin de la bêtise, du vice et de la méchanceté pour nous sentir à l'abri de leurs flèches vulgaires.

(With that oft-raised finger, those impenetrable, smiling eyes, fastened upon an unspoken enigma, you appeared to me as Leonardo's Saint John the Baptist. In those days we had a dream, almost a plan for living together, surrounded by rare, noble-minded men and women, far from stupidity, vice, and malice, and well beyond the range of their vulgar shafts.)"

Laure Hayman (1851–1932)
Odette

Proust was quite young when he fell in love with Laure Hayman, a celebrated cocotte and mistress of his Great-Uncle Louis Weil. Not long after their first meeting in the winter of 1888, Mlle Hayman gave Proust a copy of Paul Bourget's "Gladys Harvey," a story inspired by her. She had had the volume bound in silk taken from one of her petticoats. "Gladys has something of the courtesan of the eighteenth century," Bourget wrote, "and not too much of the ferociously calculating harlot of our brutal and positivist age."[1] Certainly, Hayman's lovers had been distinguished, for they included the Duc d'Orléans, the King of Greece, and Prince Karl Egon von Fürstenberg. The erotic flirtation the thirty-seven-year-old Hayman had with Marcel prompted his friend Jacques-Émile Blanche to imply later that the youth had received her ultimate favors. Proust told his housekeeper Céleste:

❝Uncle Louis was glad to give Laure Hayman anything that would make her happy. I had a great deal of admiration for her, and I spent so much on flowers for her that she warned Papa about it. He scolded me for my extravagance—I was very young. But Papa himself had some admiration for Laure Hayman on account of her sensitivity and intelligence, and he encouraged me to keep up a friendship with her because of it.❞[2]

Four years after they had first met, Proust was still sending her flowers and ardent letters: "That a woman who is merely desirable, a mere object of lust, should divide her worshippers and incite them against one another is only natural."[3]

When Louis Weil died, Proust informed Mlle Hayman in a touching note. This was followed with another expressing his appreciation for the magnificent wreath she had sent, despite the fact that, in keeping with Jewish custom, floral tributes were not expected. The wreath was delivered by a cyclist, following the flowerless cortege as it moved toward Père Lachaise. Proust's mother was so moved that she had it buried with the coffin.

In *Remembrance of Things Past*, Laure Hayman became, of course, the model for Odette, although the original was far more intelligent, witty, and cultivated than her fictional counterpart. The Narrator tells of Swann's first encounter with Odette:

❝But, whereas each of these liaisons, or each of these flirtations, had been the realisation, more or less complete, of a dream born of the sight of a face or a body which Swann had spontaneously, without effort on his part, found attractive, on the contrary when, one evening at the theatre, he was introduced to Odette de Crécy by an old friend of his, who had spoken of her as a ravishing creature with whom he might possibly come to an understanding, but had made her out to be harder of conquest than she actually was in order to appear to have done him a bigger favour by the introduction, she had struck Swann not, certainly, as being devoid of beauty, but as endowed with a kind of beauty which left him indifferent, which aroused in him no desire, which gave him, indeed, a sort of physical repulsion, as one of those women of whom all of us can cite examples, different for each of us, who are the converse of the type which our senses demand. Her profile was too sharp, her skin too delicate, her

49

cheekbones were too prominent, her features too tightly drawn, to be attractive to him. Her eyes were beautiful, but so large they seemed to droop beneath their own weight, strained the rest of her face and always made her appear unwell or in a bad mood. . . .[4]

Subsequently the Narrator gives us a view of her as Mme Swann presiding over a drawing room where "the Far East was retreating before the invading forces of the nineteenth century. . . .":

❝ *. . . Nowadays it was rarely in Japanese kimonos that Odette received her intimates, but rather in the bright and billowing silk of a Watteau housecoat whose flowering foam she would make as though to rub gently over her bosom, and in which she basked, lolled, disported herself with such an air of well-being, of cool freshness, taking such deep breaths, that she seemed to look on these garments not as something decorative, a mere setting for herself, but as necessary, in the same way as her "tub" or her daily "constitutional," to satisfy the requirements of her physiognomy and the niceties of hygiene. She used often to say that she would go without bread rather than give up art and cleanliness. . . .*

Swann had in his room, instead of the handsome photographs that were now taken of his wife, in all of which the same enigmatic and winning expression enabled one to recognise, whatever dress and hat she was wearing, her triumphant face and figure, a little daguerreotype of her, quite plain, taken long before the appearance of this new type, from which the youthfulness and beauty of Odette, which she had not yet discovered when it was taken, appeared to be missing. But doubtless Swann, having remained constant, or having reverted, to a different conception of her, enjoyed in the frail young woman with pensive eyes and tired features, caught in a pose between stillness and motion, a more Botticellian charm. . . .❞[5]

Nicolas Cottin (c. 1887–1916)

Young Nicolas Cottin, solid and peasant-like, entered Proust's service as a valet in 1907, after which he and his wife, Céline, would remain with the novelist for seven years, a period when *Remembrance of Things Past* was taking shape on pieces of paper scattered about the author's bedroom. One of Nicolas's jobs was to put the sheets in order with paper fasteners. Occasionally Proust would dictate passages to the valet-secretary, who took it down in a working-class hand. "His rigmaroles are as big a bloody bore as he is," Cottin later remarked to Céline, "but mark my words, when he's dead he'll be a success alright."[1]

Cottin kept a close watch over his master, and he even developed a chest condition similar to Proust's, which Céline attributed to the overheated bedroom. Whenever Proust had an asthmatic attack and could not speak, he would write notes to Nicolas, who kept them:

> *Since you preserve these missives for all time,*
> *Dear Nicolas, I'm forced to write in rhyme. . . .*
>
> *If not too weary is your wrist,*
> *Nicholas the nationalist*
> *Bring me milk-coffee steaming hot. . . .*[2]

In 1916 Cottin was sent to the front, where he died of pleurisy the same year.

Alfred Agostinelli
(1888–1914)
Albertine

Proust did not fall in love with the eighteen-year-old Agostinelli when he first hired him in 1907 to be his chauffeur around the countryside of Cabourg, a trip the novelist wrote up in an article for *Le Figaro* entitled "*Impressions de route en automobile.*" The relationship between Proust and the young man was complex, but it endured until 1914 when Agostinelli died in an airplane accident. After his death, the novelist asked Nadar's studio to make a copy of this photograph showing Alfred (right) and his younger brother Émile on either side of their father.

After repeating the Cabourg excursions with Agostinelli in 1908, and later taking him to Versailles, Proust discharged his driver, only to take him back in 1913 as a secretary and the typist of his novel. It was now that Proust fully realized the depth of their involvement and the jealous suffering that it would cost him.

Critics have debated the extent of the Proust-Agostinelli affair and its impact on *Remembrance of Things Past*, especially in regard

to the portrait of Albertine, a sexual transposition that masks the true story. When Alfred was killed in 1914 Proust wrote André Gide of his grief at "the death of a young man I loved probably more than all my friends," adding to the note a moving sketch of the relationship:

> He was a boy of delightful intelligence; and, moreover, it was not on account of that that I loved him. I went for a long time without perceiving this intelligence—not as long as he did, however. I discovered in him a merit marvelously incompatible with his whole station in life. I discovered it with stupefaction, but without its adding anything to the affection I already had for him. After discovering it, I merely took a little extra joy in revealing it to him. But he died before fully knowing what he was, and even before completely being what he was. The whole affair is shot through with such frightful circumstances that, already crushed as I am, I do not know how I can bear such grief.[1]

Proust memorialized his friend in a strange and moving passage in *Remembrance of Things Past*, where the Narrator is out riding on horseback in the countryside near Balbec:

> ... Suddenly my horse reared up; he had heard a strange noise, and it was only with difficulty that I got him back under control and avoided being thrown to the ground; I raised eyes filled with tears toward the point from which the noise seemed to come, and I saw, about fifty yards above me, in the sunlight, soaring between two great and shining wings of steel, a being whose indistinct face seemed to resemble that of a man. I was as overcome as an ancient Greek seeing for the first time a demigod. And I wept, for I was ready to weep from the moment I realized that the noise was coming from above my head—airplanes were still rare in those days—and at the thought that I was now going to see an airplane for the first time. As when, while reading, one senses the approach of a moving word, I was waiting only for the actual sight of the airplane before breaking into tears. But the aviator seemed to hesitate on his course. I felt opening before him—before me, if habit had not made me a prisoner—all the roads of space, all the roads of life; he flew on, glided for several seconds above the sea; then suddenly making up his mind, and seeming to yield to some force the opposite of gravity, as if he were returning to his native land, with a light movement of his golden wings, he rose into the sky.[2]

The
Guermantes
Way

Marie de Benardaky
Gilberte

I n the summer of 1886 the fourteen-year-old Marcel Proust saw Marie de Benardaky for the first time. Years later, after she had married Prince Michel Radziwill, the novelist still thought of her as "one of the two great loves of my life." Marie and her younger sister Nelly were daughters of a Polish nobleman, Nicolas de Benardaky, who had served as master of ceremonies at the court of the Tsar. The Benardaky family lived at 65 Rue de Chaillot, just west of the Champs-Élysées, where the children of that aristocratic section of Paris were taken to play. It was here, along the shaded walks of the great avenue, that Proust first encountered the elegant, tall, dark-haired Marie, who was to become the unlikely model for the red-haired and pouty Gilberte.

Young Marcel was completely captivated by Marie as each day she ran with her sister ahead of their governess to play prisoner's base in the park. The Narrator recalls the pretty, spirited Marie in his portrait of Gilberte:

❝Meanwhile Gilberte never came to the Champs-Elysées. And yet it was imperative that I should see her, for I could not so much as remember her face. The questing, anxious, exacting way that we have of looking at the person we love, our eagerness for the word which will give us or take from us the hope of an appointment for the morrow, and, until that word is uttered, our alternate if not simultaneous imaginings of joy and despair, all this makes our attention in the presence of the beloved too tremulous to be able to carry away a very clear impression of her. Perhaps, also, that activity of all the senses at once which yet endeavours to discover with the eyes alone what lies beyond them is over-indulgent to the myriad forms, to the different savours, to the movements of the living person whom as a rule, when we are not in love, we immobilise. Whereas the beloved model does not stay still; and our mental photographs of it are always blurred. I no longer really knew how Gilberte's features were composed, save in the heavenly moments when she unfolded them to me: I could remember nothing but her smile. And being unable to visualise that beloved face, despite every effort that I might make to recapture it, I was disgusted to find, etched on my memory with a maddening precision of detail, the meaningless, emphatic faces of the roundabout man and the barley-sugar woman; just as those who have lost a loved one whom they never see again in sleep, are enraged at meeting incessantly in their dreams any number of insupportable people whom it is quite enough to have known in the waking world. In their inability to form an image of the object of their grief they are almost led to accuse themselves of feeling no grief. And I was not far from believing that, since I could not recall Gilberte's features, I had forgotten Gilberte herself, and no longer loved her.❞[1]

Mme de Benardaky
Odette

Tall, beautiful Mme de Benardaky, the mother of Marie and Nelly, had the reputation of caring for nothing but champagne and love. Although the Benardakys belonged to aristocratic circles beyond the reach of the Prousts, they were not considered *gratin*. "Mme de Benardaky has reached such a high position in society," Mlle de Malakoff remarked, "that the only person you see in her house who isn't out of the top drawer is herself."[1]

When Marie, in her mother's name, invited the smitten Marcel to tea "at five o'clock, on any day you wish," he was quite overcome in his anticipation of entering the grand precincts of the Benardaky house in the Rue de Chaillot. Along with Laure Hayman and Mme Straus, Mme de Benardaky contributed to the character of Odette Swann:

❝ . . . Mme Swann attached great importance to her "tea"; she thought that she showed her originality and expressed her charm when she said to a man: "You'll find me at home any day, fairly late; come to tea," and so would accompany with a sweet and subtle smile these words which she pronounced with a fleeting trace of an English accent, and which her listener duly noted, bowing solemnly in acknowledgment, as though the invitation had been something important and uncommon which commanded deference and required attention. There was another reason, apart from those given already, for the flowers' having more than a merely ornamental significance in Mme Swann's drawing-room, and this reason pertained not to the period but, in some degree, to the life that Odette had formerly led. A great courtesan, such as she had been, lives largely for her lovers, that is to say at home, which means that she comes in time to live for her home. The things that one sees in the house of a "respectable" woman, things which may of course appear to her also to be of importance, are those which are in any event of the utmost importance to the courtesan. ❞[2]

Lt. Comte Armand de Cholet
Saint-Loup

Despite his far from robust health, Proust volunteered in 1889 for a year of military service. Even though technically in the ranks, volunteers were an élite group, educated through the *baccalauréat*, or its equivalent, and uniformed, as well as maintained in the service, at their parents' expense. They came from the *noblesse* and the *haute bourgeoisie*, which made them an homogeneous group of well-bred young men who were treated as officer cadets. For Proust, the year in the army was undoubtedly one of the happiest periods of his life. "It's curious," Proust wrote to a friend some fifteen years later, "that you should have regarded the Army as a prison, I as a paradise." And in *Les Plaisirs et les jours* he mused: ". . . the calm of a life in which occupations are more regulated and the imagination less trammeled than in any other, in which pleasure is the more constantly with us because we have no time to run about looking for it."[1]

Proust's immediate commander was Lieutenant de Cholet, a handsome young officer and member of the closed, aristocratic Parisian enclaves of the Jockey Club and the "Cercle de la Royale" who would provide some of the characteristics of Saint-Loup. At the end of the year's service, Cholet gave Proust his photograph signed "to Marcel Proust volunteer cadet, from one of his torturers." It was a print of the Nadar photograph taken in November 1888. In *Les Plaisirs et les jours* Proust refers to his military service in the section entitled "Regrets et rêveries," and in *Jean Santeuil* he includes a scene where Jean is invited to dinner by his Lieutenant, just as Proust had no doubt been invited by Cholet.

When the Narrator, in *Within a Budding Grove*, describes the occasion on which he met Saint-Loup walking with his aunt while on leave, he evokes the sentiments of Proust himself, who once encountered Cholet in the street, only to be recognized by a cold military salute:

❝ . . . *When Mme de Villeparisis, doubtless in an attempt to counteract the bad impression that had been made on us by an exterior indicative of an arrogant and unfriendly nature, spoke to us again of the inexhaustible kindness of her great-nephew (he was the son of one of her nieces, and a little older than myself), I marvelled how the gentry, with an utter disregard of truth, ascribe tenderness of heart to people whose hearts are in reality so hard and dry, provided only that they behave with common courtesy to the brilliant members of their own set. Mme de Villeparisis herself confirmed, though indirectly, my diagnosis, which was already a conviction, of the essential points of her nephew's character one day when I met them both coming along a path so narrow that she could not do otherwise than introduce me to him. He seemed not to hear that a person's name was being announced to him; not a muscle of his face moved; his eyes, in which there shone not the faintest gleam of human sympathy, showed merely, in the insensibility, in the inanity of their gaze an exaggeration failing which there would have been nothing to distinguish them from lifeless mirrors. Then, fastening on me those hard eyes as though he wished to examine me before returning my salute, with an abrupt gesture which seemed to be due rather to a reflex action of his muscles than to an exercise of will, keeping between himself and me the greatest possible interval, he stretched his arm out to its full extension and, at the end of it,*

offered me his hand. . . . *there were moments when my mind distinguished in Saint-Loup a personality more generalised than his own, that of the "nobleman," which like an indwelling spirit moved his limbs, ordered his gestures and his actions; then, at such moments, although in his company, I was alone, as I should have been in front of a landscape the harmony of which I could understand. He was no more then than an object of properties of which, in my musings, I sought to explore. The discovery in him of this pre-existent, this immemorial being, this aristocrat who was precisely what Robert aspired not to be, gave me intense joy, but a joy of the mind rather than the feelings.* [2]

Comtesse Élisabeth Greffulhe
(1860–1952)
Duchesse de Guermantes
Princesse de Guermantes

When young Marcel Proust first saw the agate-eyed Mme Greffulhe in the drawing room of Princesse Alexandre Wagram in 1893, he reacted like a lepidopterist who had sighted a rare specimen of butterfly on some far slope of the Himalayas. "I have at last (yesterday at the home of Mme de Wagram) seen the Comtesse Greffulhe and the same feeling that decided me to impart to you my emotion on reading *Les Chauves-souris* compels me to choose you as the confidant of my emotion of the evening," he wrote to his friend Robert de Montesquiou the next morning. The thirty-three-year-old wife of Henri Greffulhe (p. 74), a member of a rich Belgian banking family, was considered by everyone in Paris to be the supreme beauty of her day. "Her hair was dressed with Polynesian grace, and mauve orchids hung down the nape of her neck," Proust reported to Montesquiou, who happened to be the Countess's cousin. "It is hard to judge her, because to judge her is to compare," he continued, "and because in her there is no feature that can be found in any other woman or anywhere else." It was her remarkable eyes, he concluded, that revealed the secret of the power she held over everyone who saw her: "But the whole mystery of her beauty lies in the brilliance and especially the enigma of her eyes. I have never seen a woman more beautiful."[1]

Proust's idolatry of Mme Greffulhe was to last for years, although it would be carried on at a distance, unlike the relationships he developed with a number of his hostesses. He seemed paralyzed at that first sight of Mme Greffulhe, and could only admire and study her from across the room, fearing that a more intimate encounter (or rebuff) might break the enchantress's spell. "I didn't ask to be introduced to her and I shall not even ask you," Proust told Montesquiou, "for apart from the indiscretion that might imply, it seems to me that speaking to her would agitate me rather painfully. I would like her to know what an enormous impression she made on me, and, if, as I believe, you see her often, would you tell her?"[2] Years later, Proust wrote a sketch of her salon for *Le Figaro*, but it was never published, depriving us of a more complete picture of his feelings and impressions.

In 1949, sixty years after Proust had received his first glimpse of the heroine, an intimidated Mina Curtiss was introduced to the legendary, but now ancient, Countess while doing research on the novelist's letters. Mme Greffulhe was still a presence, one that continued to radiate a certain magic, even at the age of ninety. "I too found her eyes uniquely magnetic," Curtiss wrote in her memoirs.[3]

Provided it could be assembled, a small exhibition of the Countess's memorabilia—the portrait by Laszlo, Nadar's photograph, her Worth gowns, perhaps the huge cabochon emerald she wore on a withered finger when Mina Curtiss met her, La Gandara's drawing of her chin from Montesquiou's collection—might help us grasp something of the material quality of this goddess. For the *gratin* of Parisian society and, of course, for Proust, Mme Greffulhe exuded the sort of glamour and beauty that must have been a Belle Époque equivalent of the allure attributed to the great film queens of Hollywood. If a rumor circulated that the Countess had just been seen at a gala, every guest would urgently ask "Which way did she go? Which way did she go?" hoping to catch even a fleeting glimpse.

"One does not meet her about any more than one meets the Archbishop of Paris," her admirer Élisabeth de Gramont remarked. "Like Salambô, she never shows herself to the crowd except from the top of a staircase, or surrounded by Kings, if there are any to be had. . . . "

Although for her role as a prototype of the Duchesse *and* the Princesse de Guermantes, Mme Greffulhe will forever be associated with Proust and his circle, the

Countess actually saw very little of the novelist. She told Miss Curtiss that she included him in her larger guest list only to please her cousin Robert, and thus invited "him a few times to soirées where he could mingle with the sort of people he wanted to meet." But, she confided, she could not stand him: "His sticky flattery was not to my taste. There was something I found unattractive about him. And then there was the nonsense about my photograph, pestering Robert to get one from me." At this point, the venerable aristocrat recalled the special feeling people had about photographs, a feeling that Proust's mother also expressed on at least one occasion to her son. "In those days, Madame," the Countess explained to Miss Curtiss, "photographs were considered private and intimate. One didn't give them to outsiders." Poor Marcel, to think he once said her laughter sounded "like the chimes of Bruges." He never seemed to get the message, and even at the wedding of the Greffulhes' daughter to his friend the Duc de Guiche, the Countess could hardly hide her irritation when the importunate author again mentioned the photograph to her as she left the church. "He was tiresome," she recalled with an exasperation that had not faded with the years.[4]

In her memoirs, Proust's housekeeper Céleste, with naïve but acute perception, said that the writer wanted his characters to be "perfect" in their individual composition. And the image and manners of Mme Greffulhe projected the perfection—the quintessential type—that he was seeking to embody in the character of his ideal Faubourg Saint-Germain Duchess, the Duchesse de Guermantes. It is this general quality, rather than the many specific details that Proust gives us in his description of the Guermantes world, that evokes the lingering memory of the once-celebrated beauty.

Because another brilliant lady of the period, Mme de Chevigné (see p. 65), also figures in the composition of the Duchesse de Guermantes's personality and life, it is difficult to be too explicit about who made individual contributions. In the case of both Mme Greffulhe and Mme de Chevigné, Proust was fascinated from an early age. And just as he would stand in the Champs-Élysées and the Avenue Marigny to wait for Mme de Chevigné to drive by in her carriage, so he would go to the Opéra just to see Mme Greffulhe ascend Garnier's great staircase.

In the drawing room of Mme de Villeparisis, the Narrator confesses how, with his mother's help, he was finally able to break the exhausting enchantment the Duchess had cast over him when he sees

❛ . . . *emerging, majestic, ample and tall in a flowing gown of yellow satin upon which huge black poppies were picked out in relief, the Duchess herself. The sight of her no longer disturbed me in the least. One fine day my mother, laying her hands on my forehead (as was her habit when she was afraid of hurting my feelings) and saying: "You really must stop hanging about trying to meet Mme de Guermantes. You're becoming a laughing-stock. Besides, look how ill your grandmother is, you really have something more serious to think about than waylaying a woman who doesn't care a straw about you," instantaneously—like a hypnotist who brings you back from the distant country in which you imagined yourself to be, and opens your eyes for you, or like the doctor who, by recalling you to a sense of duty and reality, cures you of an imaginary disease in which you have been wallowing—had awakened me from an unduly protracted dream. The rest of the day had been consecrated to a last farewell to this malady which I was renouncing; I had sung, for hours on end and weeping as I sang, the sad words of Schubert's* Adieu:

*Farewell, strange voices call thee
Away from me, dear sister of the angels.* ❜[5]

64

Comtesse Laure de Chevigné
(1860–1936)
Duchesse de Guermantes

Born into the provincial *noblesse*, Laure de Sade was rather proud of her connection with the notorious Marquis de Sade, although the name was not one to place her on the same exalted level with the Duchesse de Guermantes, for whom she served as one of Proust's chief models. In 1879 Mlle de Sade had married Comte Adhéaume de Chevigné, gentleman-in-waiting to Comte de Chambord, the Bourbon pretender to the throne of

France. These legendary connections and her own natural dignity and grace were enough to provide at least some inspiration for the unforgettable portrait that Proust would draw of the Duchesse de Guermantes. But Mme de Chevigné had fascinated the novelist long before he conceived of the Duchess as she appears in Parisian society, at Mme Lemaire's parties, at the Opéra, and walking in the Champs-Élysées. As early as 1892 young Proust had used the Countess for a sketch published in *Le Banquet*, where she appears as Hippolyta, a birdlike Italian beauty elegantly seated in a theater box, her white gauze dress falling about her like folded wings, with a white feather fan completing the goddess-bird image.

The Duchesse de Guermantes makes her first appearance in the church at Combray, seated in the family chapel of Gilbert the Bad and surrounded by the tombs of her ancestors:

❝*I felt it to be important that she should not leave the church before I had been able to look at her for long enough, reminding myself that for years past I had regarded the sight of her as a thing eminently to be desired, and I kept my eyes fixed on her, . . .*

I can see her still quite clearly, especially at the moment when the procession filed into the sacristy, which was lit up by the intermittent warm sunshine of a windy and rainy day and in which Mme de Guermantes found herself in the midst of all those Combray people whose names she did not even know, but whose inferiority proclaimed her own supremacy too loudly for her not to feel sincerely benevolent towards them, and whom she might count on impressing even more forcibly by virtue of her simplicity and graciousness. . . . I can still see, above her mauve scarf, puffed and silky, the gentle astonishment in her eyes, to which she had added, without daring to address it to anyone in particular, but so that everyone might enjoy his share of it, a rather shy smile as of a sovereign lady who seems to be making an apology for her presence among the vassals whom she loves. This smile fell upon me, who had never taken my eyes off her. And remembering the glance which she had let fall upon me during mass, blue as a ray of sunlight that had penetrated the window of Gilbert the Bad, I said to myself: "She must have taken notice of me." I fancied that I had found favour in her eyes, that she would continue to think of me after she had left the church, and would perhaps feel sad that evening, at Guermantes, because of me. And at once I fell in love with her, . . .❞[1]

Duc Armand de Guiche (1879–1962)
Saint-Loup

Guiche counted among those young grandees—Albufera, Radziwill, the Bibesco brothers—whom Proust made his friends, enjoyed, and valued for their worldly knowledge, good looks, and manners. He met the tall sportsman and scientist—polo champion and international authority on optics and aerodynamics—at Anna de Noailles's in 1903. Guiche, through his mother, the Duchesse de Gramont (*née* Rothschild), was, like Proust, half Jewish, even though he bore one of the most exalted titles in France. He married the

daughter of the Comte and Comtesse Greffulhe. Inscribing a copy of *Les Plaisirs et les jours* for Armand de Guiche, the author wrote: "To the Duc de Guiche, the true one rather than the real one, the one who might have been rather than the one who is. . . . I offer this portrait, now so poor a likeness, of a Marcel he has never known."[1]

Marquis Boni de Castellane (1867–1932)
Saint-Loup

Within the Castellane and Talleyrand-Périgord families Proust found a great many details for the structure and characteristics of individual members of his great, eccentric Guermantes clan. Boni de Castellane, nephew of the Prince de Sagan, provided one of the role models for the Duc de Guermantes's nephew, Saint-Loup, even though the novelist denied it in a letter to Robert de Montesquiou, insisting that his friends and acquaintances offered "no key whatsoever" to Saint-Loup's personality.

When Boni ran out of the money necessary to support his extravagant career as a dashing man-about-town, he married the short, plain American heiress Anna Gould, and thereby gained access to a great fortune. With his finances thus replenished, the Marquis proceeded to design and build the famous Palais de Marbre Rose, a grand, sumptuous house modeled on the Petit Trianon at Versailles and located on the ultra-fashionable Avenue du Bois. There the Gould money enabled him to hold receptions and parties whose brilliance and lavishness made Boni de Castellane the most talked about figure in Parisian society. At the famous ball of 1897, given in celebration of Mme de Castellane's twenty-first birthday, three thousand guests, including Proust, were invited and entertained at a cost of 300,000 francs, some of which went to pay for a performance by the entire corps de ballet from the Paris Opéra.

With his elegance, hauteur, golden hair, cold blue eyes, and tall, fast-moving figure, Boni possessed physical characteristics that made him an unmistakable prototype of Proust's Saint-Loup. In *Within a Budding Grove*, the Narrator recalls seeing Saint-Loup, the nephew of Mme de Villeparisis, at a seaside resort hotel.

❝One afternoon of scorching heat I was in the dining-room of the hotel, plunged in semi-darkness to shield it from the sun, which gilded the drawn curtains through the gaps between which twinkled the blue of the sea, when along the central gangway leading from the beach to the road I saw approaching, tall, slim, bare-necked, his head held proudly erect, a young man with searching eyes whose skin was as fair and his hair as golden as if they had absorbed all the rays of the sun. Dressed in a suit of soft, whitish material such as I could never have believed that any man would have the audacity to wear, the thinness of which suggested no less vividly than the coolness of the dining-room the heat and brightness of the glorious day outside, he was walking fast. His penetrating eyes, from one of which a monocle kept dropping, were the colour of the sea. Everyone looked at him with interest as he passed, knowing that this young Marquis de Saint-Loup-en-Bray was famed for his elegance. All the newspapers had described the suit in which he had recently acted as second to the young Duc d'Uzès in a duel. One felt that the distinctive quality of his hair, his eyes, his skin, his bearing, which would have marked him out in a crowd like a precious vein of opal, azure-shot and luminous, embedded in a mass of coarser substance, must correspond to a life different from that led by other men. So that when, before the attachment which Mme de Villeparisis had been deploring, the prettiest women in society had disputed the possession of him, his presence, at a watering-place for instance, in the company of the beauty of the season to whom he was paying court, not only brought her into the limelight, but attracted every eye fully as much to himself. Because of his "tone," because he had the insolent manner of a young "blood," above all because of his extraordinary good looks, some even thought him effeminate-looking, though without holding it against him since they knew how virile he was and how passionately fond of women. This was the nephew about whom Mme de Villeparisis had spoken to us. I was delighted at the thought that I was going to enjoy his company for some weeks, and confident that he would bestow on me all his affection. He strode rapidly across the whole width of the hotel, seeming to be in pursuit of his monocle, which kept darting away in front of him like a butterfly . . . .A carriage and pair awaited him at the door; and, while his monocle resumed its gambollings on the sunlit road, with the elegance and mastery which a great pianist contrives to display in the simplest stroke of execution. . . .Mme de Villeparisis's nephew, taking the reins that were handed him by the coachman, sat down beside him and, while opening a letter which the manager of the hotel brought out to him, started up his horses.❞ [1]

Marquise Boni de Castellane
(*née* Anna Gould)

Homely, firm-mouthed, disagreeable, and the daughter of an American millionaire, Anna Gould was married in 1895 to Boni de Castellane, whose fashionable world gossiped about the heiress's dowdy looks and the distinctive line of black hair that grew down her spine. Even with her new makeup and the depilation ordered by her husband, the American Marquise made an awkward addition to the glamorous Castellane parties.

After suffering repeated indignities at the hands of her huband, not to mention his infidelities, Anna took their two sons and abruptly left the Marquis in 1906. Two years later she acquired an even grander title by marrying Boni's cousin, Hélie de Talleyrand-Périgord, Prince de Sagan. A little later, Proust was introduced to the Prince and the Duc de Brissac. Confusing the two men, he made an unkind remark about Mme de Talleyrand to her husband. "How exquisitely witty, I shall tell my wife," the Prince replied. "But I don't think it could possibly interest Mme de Brissac," said Proust, making matters even worse. It was only after he had seen the initials inside the Prince's hat that he realized his blunder. Proust then restaged it in a scene between the Narrator and Charlus after Mme de Villeparisis's matinée.[1]

Vicomte Robert d'Humières
(1868–1915)
Saint-Loup

Translator of Kipling and Conrad, the handsome Robert d'Humières moved in the same circles as Proust and helped the novelist with his work on Ruskin's *The Bible of Amiens*. Humières's aristocratic good looks and some aspects of his life fit the portrait that Proust drew of Saint-Loup, including the fictional character's heroic death. Humières was killed in 1915 while leading a Zouave regiment at the front line of France's defense against the German invasion:

❝My departure from Paris was delayed by a piece of news which caused me such grief that I was for some time rendered incapable of travelling. This was the death of Robert de Saint-Loup, killed two days after his return to the front while covering the retreat of his men. Never had any man felt less hatred for a nation than he (and as for the Emperor, for particular reasons, very possibly incorrect, he thought that William II had tried rather to prevent the war than to bring it about). Nor had he hated Germanism; the last words which I had heard on his lips, six days before he died, were the opening words of a Schumann song which he had started to hum in German on my staircase, until I had made him desist because of the neighbours. Accustomed by supreme good breeding to eliminate from his conduct all trace of apology or invective, all rhetoric, he had avoided in face of the enemy, as he had at the time of mobilisation, the actions which would have ensured his survival, through that tendency to efface himself before others of which all his behaviour was symbolic, down to his manner of coming out into the street bare-headed to close the door of my cab, every time I visited him. For several days I remained shut up in my room, thinking of him. I recalled his arrival the first time at Balbec, when, in an almost white suit, with his eyes greenish and mobile like the waves, he had crossed the hall adjoining the great dining-room whose windows gave on to the sea. I recalled the very special being that he had then seemed to me to be, the being for whose friendship I had so greatly wished. That wish had been realised beyond the limits of what I should ever have thought possible, without, however, at the time giving me more than a very slight pleasure; and then later I had come to understand the many great virtues and something else as well which lay concealed behind his elegant appearance. All this, the good as well as the bad, he had given without counting the cost, every day, as much on the last day when he advanced to attack a trench, out of generosity and because it was his habit to place at the service of others all that he possessed, as on that evening when he had run along the backs of the seats in the restaurant in order not to disturb me. . . .❞[1]

Comtesse de Martel (1849–1932)
Gilberte

Great-grand-niece of Mirabeau and a friend of Proust's mother, the spirited Comtesse de Martel was better known by the name under which she wrote: Gyp. She first saw Marcel as a young boy playing in the Champs-Élysées with Antoinette Faure, who no doubt also figured in the character of Gilberte, although to a lesser degree than Marie de Benardaky.

A few days after she had seen the children playing, Comtesse de Martel was amused and surprised to see the precocious Marcel in Calmann Lévy's bookshop buying the complete works of Molière and Lamartine.

Comte Henri Greffulhe (1844–1932)
Duc de Guermantes

Scion of a Belgian banking family, the tall, imposing Comte Henri Greffulhe and his wife, the former Princesse Élisabeth de Caraman-Chimay, gave Proust his main inspiration for the Duc and Duchesse de Guermantes, the leading figures of society in *Remembrance of Things Past*. In his bluff, lordly manner, and especially in his patronizing attitude toward the electorate he represented in the Chamber of Deputies, Comte Greffulhe would seem to have been a French version of the traditional English squire. "He displaces more air than any normal mortal," remarked one acquaintance, and in Nadar's photograph, he exudes that confident, almost Renaissance quality of openness seen in certain Italian portraits. The arrogant, worldly face, the bearing and condescending courtesy have about them a kind of magnetism that surely attracted Proust in his research on the demi-deities of the Parisian upper crust. For Proust's Narrator, the doorway of the Guermantes's house represented the entry into that mysterious world:

6 *. . . It is true that my mind was perplexed by certain difficulties, and the presence of the body of Jesus Christ in the host seemed to me no more obscure a mystery than this leading house in the Faubourg being situated on the right bank of the river and so near that from my bedroom in the morning I could hear its carpets being beaten. But the line of demarcation that separated me from the Faubourg Saint-Germain seemed to me all the more real because it was purely ideal; I sensed that it was already part of the Faubourg when I saw, spread out on the other side of that Equator, the Guermantes doormat of which my mother had ventured to say, having like myself caught a glimpse of it one day when their door stood open, that it was in a shocking state. Besides, how could their dining-room, their dim gallery upholstered in red plush, into which I could see sometimes from our kitchen window, have failed to possess in my eyes the mysterious charm of the Faubourg Saint-Germain, to form an essential part of it, to be geographically situated within it, since to have been entertained to dinner in that dining-room was to have gone into the Faubourg Saint-Germain, to have breathed its atmosphere, . . . ?*

But if the Hôtel de Guermantes began for me at its hall-door, its dependencies must be regarded as extending a long way further, in the estimation of the Duke, who, looking on all the tenants as peasants, yokels, appropriators of national assets, whose opinion was of no account, shaved himself every morning in his nightshirt at the window, came down into the courtyard, according to the warmth or coldness of the day, in his shirt-sleeves, in pyjamas, in a plaid jacket of startling colours with a shaggy nap, in little light-coloured covert coats shorter than his jacket, and made one of his grooms lead past him at a trot some horse that he had just bought. . . . After seeing how a new acquisition trotted by itself he would have it harnessed and taken through all the neighbouring streets, the groom running beside the carriage holding the reins, making it pass to and fro before the Duke who stood on the pavement, erect, gigantic, enormous in his vivid clothes, a cigar between his teeth, his head in the air, his eyeglass quizzical, until the moment when he sprang on to the box, drove the horse up and down for a little to try it, then set off with his new turn-out to pick up his mistress in the Champs-Elysées. . . . 9 [1]

Comte Robert de Montesquiou
(1855–1921)
Charlus

An extraordinary figure in the Parisian society of his time, Robert de Montesquiou gave Proust one of his models for the Baron de Charlus. Of all Proust's aristocratic friends, Montesquiou could lay claim to the most eminent and the oldest of feudal connections, stretching back to the Merovingian Kings of France. The family name appears in the memoirs of Saint-Simon, and the family Château d'Artagnan still belonged to the descendants of its original builders. Montesquiou would occasionally use it as a retreat from his exhausting social life in the capital. Through marriage, he was related to most of the ducal families of France, and like Charlus, he often spoke of "my cousins the La Rochefoucaulds," "my cousins the Rohan-Chabots and my kinsmen the de Gramonts." Anatole France detested these constant references to ancestry, and Charles Haas could perfectly mimic the Count's *gratin* drawl: "My forebears used up all the intelligence; my father had nothing left but the sense of his own grandeur; my brother hadn't even that, but had the decency to die young; while I—I have added to our ducal coronet the glorious coronal of a poet."[1] In the event a hostess admired one of his frequent recitations of his own verse, Montesquiou would immediately second her judgment and proceed to repeat the performance.

Tall, thin, and hawklike, just as in the Nadar portrait, Montesquiou insisted that he looked like a greyhound in an overcoat. Proust once annoyed the Count by comparing his delicately rouged cheeks to a moss rose. In the sterile world of the Faubourg Saint-Germain, however, the eccentric aristocrat made a brilliant, comic, and utterly original presence. His world extended beyond that closed realm, for he could count among his friends such artists and writers as Mallarmé, Edmond de Goncourt, Verlaine, Gustave Moreau, Degas, Whistler, and Forain. As the Nadar portrait reveals, and as George Painter has pointed out, Montesquiou in his ultimate personification had modeled his coiffure, mustache, and stance on Whistler.[2] He had also appropriated the American painter's peculiar laugh, high, trumpet-like, and delivered with head thrown back, as well as his witty epigrams and "gentle art of making enemies."[3] Such a personality fascinated Proust, but his interest in Montesquiou was primarily aesthetic and social.

At a party given by the Verdurins, the host had tried to patronize Charlus, his social superior, by reassuring the Baron that he was "one of us" as an apology for having seated a Marquis in the place of honor. To the bourgeois Verdurin's explanation, a dismayed Charlus . . .

❝ . . . *gave a little laugh that was all his own—a laugh that came down to him probably from some Bavarian or Lorraine grandmother, who herself had inherited it, in identical form, from an ancestress, so that it had tinkled now, unchanged, for a good many centuries in little old-fashioned European courts, and one could appreciate its precious quality, like that of certain old musical instruments that have become very rare. There are times when, to paint a complete portrait of someone, we should have to add a phonetic imitation to our verbal description, and our portrait of the figure that M. de Charlus presented is liable to remain incomplete in the absence of that little laugh, so delicate, so light, just as certain works of Bach are never accurately rendered because*

our orchestras lack those small, high trumpets, with a sound so entirely their own, for which the composer wrote this or that part. . . .

"Pardon me," M. de Charlus haughtily replied to the astonished Verdurin, "I am also Duke of Brabant, Squire of Montargis, Prince of Oléron, of Carency, of Viareggio and of the Dunes. However, it's not of the slightest importance. Please don't distress yourself," he concluded, resuming his delicate smile which blossomed at these final words: "I could see at a glance that you were out of your depth". [4]

Prince Boson de Sagan
Charlus

No figure in Belle Époque Paris surpassed the Prince de Sagan in elegance and personal style. Dressed by the best tailors and forever sporting a white rose in his buttonhole, Sagan provided the era with a sumptuous archetype as he joined his friends Robert de Fitz-James, General de Galliffet, Charles Haas, and the Comte de Turenne to attend a performance at the Comédie Française. In 1908 Sagan suffered a stroke, and it was as a bent, drooling old man pushed about in a wheelchair, mumbling and bowing to the wrong people, that Proust remembered him in the image of a dying Baron de Charlus:

❝ . . . M. de Charlus, now convalescent after an attack of apoplexy of which I had had no knowledge (I had only been told that he had lost his sight, but in fact this trouble had been purely temporary and he could now see quite well again) and which, unless the truth was that hitherto he had dyed his hair and that he had now been forbidden to continue so fatiguing a practice, had had the effect, as in a sort of chemical precipitation, of rendering visible and brilliant all that saturation of metal which the locks of his hair and his beard, pure silver now, shot forth like so many geysers, so that upon the old fallen prince this latest illness had conferred the Shakespearian majesty of a King Lear. His eyes had not remained unaffected by this total convulsion, this metallurgical transformation of his head, but had, by an inverse phenomenon, lost all their brightness. But what was most moving was that one felt that this lost brightness was identical with his moral pride, and that somehow the physical and even the intellectual life of M. de Charlus had survived the eclipse of that aristocratic haughtiness which had in the past seemed indissolubly linked to them. To confirm this, at the moment which I am describing, there passed in a victoria, no doubt also on her way to the reception of the Prince de Guermantes, Mme de Saint-Euverte, whom formerly the Baron had not considered elegant enough for him. Jupien, who tended him like a child, whispered in his ear that it was someone with whom he was acquainted, Mme de Saint-Euverte. And immediately, with infinite laboriousness but with all the concentration of a sick man determined to show that he is capable of all the movements which are still difficult for him, M. de Charlus lifted his hat, bowed, and greeted Mme de Saint-Euverte as respectfully as if she had been the Queen of France or as if he had been a small child coming timidly in obedience to his mother's command to say "How do you do?" to a grown-up person. For a child, but without a child's pride, was what he had once more become. . . . ❞ [1]

Comte Louis de Turenne
Bréauté

As photographed by Nadar, the Comte de Turenne, with his monocle, top hat, and cane, could almost be an actor impersonating the typical Faubourg aristocrat. But Turenne was authentic, and, along with Comte Henri de Breteuil, he became the prototype for Hannibal (Babal) de Bréauté, whose own monocle "carried, glued to the other side, an infinitesimal gaze, swarming with affability, and never ceasing to beam at the height of the ceiling, the magnificence of the reception, the interestingness of the program and the quality of the refreshments."[1]

Turenne and the painter Detaille were the only other guests at the celebrated dinner party given by Comtesse Greffulhe for Edward VII and Queen Alexandra in 1910. Proust re-created the occasion in *The Guermantes Way*, with the Duchess as hostess:

While I was being introduced to the ladies, one of the gentlemen of the party had been showing various signs of agitation: this was Comte Hannibal de Bréauté-Consalvi. Having arrived late, he had not had time to investigate the composition of the party, and when I entered the room, seeing in me a guest who was not one of the Duchess's regular circle and must therefore have some quite extraordinary claim to admission, installed his monocle beneath the groined arch of his eyebrow, thinking that this would help him, far more than to see me, to discern what manner of man I was. He knew that Mme de Guermantes had (the priceless appanage of truly superior women) what was called a "salon," that is to say added occasionally to the people of her own set some celebrity who had recently come into prominence by the discovery of a new cure for something or the production of a masterpiece. The Faubourg Saint-Germain had not yet recovered from the shock of learning that the Duchess had not been afraid to invite M. Detaille to the reception which she had given to meet the King and Queen of England. The clever women of the Faubourg were not easily consolable for not having been invited, so deliciously thrilling would it have been to come into contact with that strange genius. . . . [2]

Costume Ball of the Princesse de Léon

The famous "ball of the Princesse de Léon" (pp. 82–83) was given before the hostess's husband had inherited the illustrious title of Duc de Rohan-Chabot. The Princess is, of course, seated at the center of her "court," while Boni de Castellane, richly dressed as the Maréchal de Saxe in a sable-trimmed purple cloak, stands second from the right.

One of the celebrated Guermantes hostesses, the Princesse de Léon accepted so many people into her salon that the throng once forced her daughter, Marie Murat, to communicate with the Princess through a message to the butler: "Tell Mother I couldn't get to her through all of those poets." The absent-minded Princess invited Verlaine to a reception several years after the poet had died. When a guest complained that another guest had just gotten out of prison, the hostess ignored the warning and replied: "Oh, poor dear, no wonder he looks so sad!"[1]

Swann mentions the Princess's ball, and Mme de Guermantes tells an anecdote of her relative the Princess's husband:

On one occasion when I asked Mme de Guermantes who a young blood was whom she had introduced to me as her nephew but whose name I had failed to catch, I was none the wiser when from the back of her throat the Duchess uttered in a very loud but quite inarticulate voice: 'C'est l' . . . i Eon . . . l . . . b . . . frère à Roert. He claims to have the same shape of skull as the ancient Welsh." Then I realized that she had said: "C'est le petit Léon," and that this was the Prince de Léon, who was indeed Robert de Saint-Loup's brother-in-law. "I know nothing about his skull," she went on, "but the way he dresses, and I must say he does dress very well, is not at all in the style of those parts. . . . [2]

Marquise de Brantes (1842–1914)

Devoted friend and correspondent, the Marquise de Brantes sent at least one picture of herself to Proust, who replied: "This fine photograph, which my imagination retouches to the point of perfect resemblance, which my memory varies with one or another hair-do or gown, has given me the greatest pleasure and I thank you for it with all my heart."[1]

Proust felt sure enough of Mme de Brantes's broad-minded hospitality to introduce his friend Reynaldo Hahn into her drawing room. Her nephew remarked that the liberality practiced by the Marquise was "worth a whole Council of Trent."[2] Rich, charming, and malicious, she accepted, along with others from the Faubourg, Proust's invitation to dinner at 45 Rue de Courcelles and later at the Ritz.

Princesse Mathilde (1820–1904)

As a niece of Napoleon I, Princesse Mathilde presided over a brilliant Second Empire salon frequented by Flaubert, Renan, Sainte-Beuve, Taine, Dumas *fils*, Mérimée, and the Goncourt brothers. By the time Proust met her, she was in her seventies, and although no longer "Notre Dame des Arts," the Princess still attracted a fashionable circle that included the Strauses, Charles Haas, Dr. Pozzi, and Counts Benedetti and Primoli.

Short and plump, Princesse Mathilde resembled her uncle, the great Emperor, and in her manner and voice, she affected a gruff Bonaparte presence. When officially invited to accompany Tsar Nicholas II to Napoleon's tomb, at the Invalides, she declined the honor saying that she had her own keys.

The Princess appears as herself in *Remembrance of Things Past*, but she also provided a few details for the personality of the Princesse de Parme.

The Swanns, accompanied by the Narrator, meet Princesse Mathilde in the Bois:

❝ . . . The old lady, who was now within a few yards of us, smiled at us with a caressing sweetness. Swann doffed his hat. Mme Swann swept to the ground in a curtsey and made as if to kiss the hand of the lady, who, standing there like a Winterhalter portrait, drew her up again and kissed her cheek. "Come, come, will you put your hat on, you!" she scolded Swann in a thick and almost growling voice, speaking like an old and familiar friend. "I'm going to present you to Her Imperial Highness," Mme Swann whispered.

Swann drew me aside for a moment while his wife talked to the Princess about the weather and the animals recently added to the Zoo. "That is the Princesse Mathilde," he told me, "you know who I mean, the friend of Flaubert, Sainte-Beuve, Dumas. Just fancy, she's the niece of Napoleon I. She had offers of marriage from Napoleon III and the Emperor of Russia. Isn't that interesting? Talk to her a little. But I hope she won't keep us standing here for an hour! . . . I met Taine the other day," he went on, addressing the Princess, "and he told me your Highness was vexed with him." "He's behaved like a perfect peeg!" she said gruffly, pronouncing the word cochon as though she referred to Joan of Arc's contemporary, Bishop Cauchon. "After his article on the Emperor I left my card on him with p. p. c. on it."

I felt the surprise that one feels on opening the correspondence of that Duchesse d'Orléans who was by birth a Princess Palatine. And indeed Princesse Mathilde, animated by sentiments so entirely French, expressed them with a straightforward bluntness that recalled the Germany of an older generation, and was inherited, doubtless, from her Württemberger mother. This somewhat rough and almost masculine frankness she softened, as soon as she began to smile, with an Italian languor. And the whole person was clothed in an outfit so typically Second Empire that—for all that the Princess wore it simply and solely, no doubt, from attachment to the fashions that she had loved when she was young—she seemed to have deliberately planned to avoid the slightest discrepancy in historic colour, and to be satisfying the expectations of those who looked to her to evoke the memory of another age. . . . ❞[1]

Edward, Prince of Wales (1841–1910)

Queen Victoria's eldest son was completely at home in Paris, a city he had first known as a young man. Moreover, his presence there lent a definite tone to the upper reaches of the *gratin* that so fascinated Proust. Not only was His Royal Highness a close companion of Charles Haas, the model for Proust's Swann, but he also accepted to be the guest of honor at a small dinner given by the Comtesse Greffulhe, an occasion that Proust re-creates at the house of the Duchess in *The Guermantes Way*.

For Proust, as for the Faubourg Saint-Germain, the heir first in line of succession to an actual throne brought an aura of historical reality to Paris's royalist circles, a quality that could not be supplied by pretenders or French titles with no claim to political power. In *Pastiches et mélanges*, Proust satirizes this sense of loss by shifting the scene of a state

visit made by the King of England to the France of Saint-Simon at Saint-Cloud in the seventeenth century:

❝ *The supper was served by Olivier, the King's head butler, his name was Dabescat[1]; he was respectful, liked by all and so well known by everyone at the English court that many of the lords who accompanied the King were more pleased to see him than the unfamiliar faces of the knights of Saint-Louis, recently created by the Regent. He was very faithful to the memory of the late king and went each year to the mass said for him at Saint-Denis where to the shame of the forgetful courtiers, he found himself almost always alone with me. I mention him in passing because, by his perfect knowledge of his position, his kindness and his connection with the great ones (without familiarity or servility) had given importance at Saint-Cloud and made him an unusual character there.*

The Regent made a very true remark to Madame Standish[2] that she did not wear her pearls like other women but in a way that the Queen of England had imitated. ❞[3]

Princesse Hélène Soutzo

Beautiful, amusing, and Roumanian-Greek, Hélène Soutzo was introduced to Proust at Larue's by his friend the writer Paul Morand, who would later marry the Princesse. Proust "studied her black wrap and ermine muff like an entomologist absorbed in the nervures of a firefly's wing, while the waiters fluttered in circles around him," Morand recalled.[1] As it turned out, Princesse Soutzo was the last young woman in Parisian society to capture the novelist's devotion ("the only woman who, to my misfortune, has succeeded in making me leave my retirement"). At her invitation Proust dined with Soutzo and friends at the Ritz in the spring of 1917, thereupon giving birth to his final image. As "Proust of the Ritz," he dined there several times a week, finding in the great hotel a perfect miniature world of friends and acquaintances, all presided over by the sinister head waiter Olivier Dabescat, who whispered every kind of gossip in the ear of the attentive guest seated at the best table.

After the shelling of Paris on the night of July 27, 1917, all the while that Proust dined with Morand and Princesse Soutzo, the novelist wrote her: "I am not afraid of the cannons and gothas but I am afraid of much less dangerous things, such as mice."[2] In *Time Regained*, the Narrator takes refuge in Jupien's hotel—actually a male brothel—during one of the German raids. His observations on its inmates recall the letter to Princesse Soutzo:

❝ *... Indeed, the threat of physical danger delivered them from the fear which for long had morbidly harassed them. For it is wrong to suppose that the scale of our fears corresponds to that of the dangers by which they are inspired. A man may be afraid of not sleeping and not in the least afraid of a serious duel, afraid of a rat and not of a lion. . . .* ❞[3]

Prince Constantin Radziwill
Prince de Guermantes

When it came to matters of birth and etiquette, the Prince de Guermantes in the "almost fossil rigidity of his aristocratic prejudice" was even more feudal than his cousin the Duke.[1] Prince Radziwill hoarded a generous provision of the same antique attitudes. An ancient family, the Radziwills were widely connected not only in Poland but also throughout Europe, and Constantin's branch reached well into the heart of French aristocracy. Léon Radziwill, Constantin's son and a friend of Proust's, complained that in Poland one said "you Frenchmen," and in France one jeered, "you Poles!" When the Prince's sister-in-law was taken to the Ritz by her nephew, Boni de Castellane, she declared: "I am particularly grateful to you for taking me to that inn, my dear, because I have never dined in an inn before."[2]

Prince Constantin maintained a celebrated staff of twelve handsome footmen, to each of whom he once gave a present of a pearl necklace. The arrangement drew a bit of poetic acid from the pen of the lethally witty Comte de Montesquiou: "It is most uncivil/To mention ladies to Constantin Radziwill." Thus, the Polish aristocrat served as a prototype for the Prince de Guermantes not only in his antediluvian snobbery but also in his later homosexual phase. To Montesquiou he admitted: "Taking the good years with the bad, blackmail costs me 70,000 francs a year."[3] Something of this candor surfaces in the character of the Prince de Guermantes as presented in *Time Regained*:

Bloch asked me to introduce him to the Prince de Guermantes, and this operation raised for me not a shadow of those difficulties which I had come up against on the day when I went to an evening party at his house for the first time, difficulties which had then seemed to me a part of the natural order whereas now I found it the simplest thing in the world to introduce to the Prince a guest whom he had invited himself and I should even have ventured, without warning, to bring to his party and introduce to him someone whom he had not invited. Was this because, since that distant era, I had become an intimate member, though for a long time now a forgotten one, of that fashionable world in which I had then been so new? Was it, on the contrary, because I did not really belong to that world, so that all the imaginary difficulties which beset people in society no longer existed for me once my shyness had vanished? Was it because, having gradually come to see what lay behind the first (and often the second and even the third) artificial appearance of others, I sensed behind the haughty disdain of the Prince a great human avidity to know people, to make the acquaintance even of those whom he affected to despise? Was it also because the Prince himself had changed, like so many men in whom the arrogance of their youth and of their middle years is tempered by the gentleness of old age—particularly as the new men and the unknown ideas whose progress they had once resisted are now familiar to them, at least by sight, and they see that they are accepted all round them in society—a change which takes place more effectually if old age is assisted in its task by some good quality or some vice in the individual which enlarges the circle of his acquaintance, or by the revolution wrought by a political conversion such as that of the Prince to Dreyfusism?[4]

General Marquis Gaston de Galliffet (1830–1909)
General de Froberville

A dashing military figure, General de Galliffet had led the famous cavalry charge at Sédan, the climactic moment of the brief Franco-Prussian War of 1870, and had participated directly in the bloody suppression of the Commune in Paris the year Proust was born (1871). With society ladies General de Galliffet had become a legendary success, some of which, it was said, could be attributed to curiosity about the actual size of a silver plate he wore in his abdomen, a souvenir of a wound received in the Battle of Puebla in the 1863 Mexican Expedition. At the height of the Dreyfus Affair, he became Minister of War in 1899 and set about decisively to bring an end to that dolorous episode, even if it meant suppressing his personal sentiments in order to see that justice was done.[1]

Galliffet belonged to a fashionable circle that included the Prince de Sagan, Charles Haas, and the Comte de Turenne, all of whom appear in Tissot's painting *Le Cercle de la Rue Royale*. When the General married a Laffitte, the guests at the wedding could not suppress their laughter upon hearing the priest speak the words: "When the inevitable hour of separation comes."[2] But Galliffet had a notable wit of his own, a quality that endeared him to Proust. By way of example, George Painter reports that while riding in the Bois one afternoon the General came upon the unfrocked priest who had been chaplain to the Empress Eugénie. As the former cleric tipped his hat, Galliffet returned the courtesy by making the sign of priestly benediction.[3]

In *Swann's Way* Galliffet appears briefly as General de Froberville at a soirée given by the Marquise de Saint-Euverte:

❝*Swan speedily recovered his sense of the general ugliness of the human male when, on the other side of the tapestry curtain, the spectacle of the servants gave place to that of the guests. But even this ugliness of faces which of course were mostly familiar to him seemed something new now that their features—instead of being to him symbols of practical utility in the identification of this or that person who until then had represented merely so many pleasures to be pursued, boredoms to be avoided, or courtesies to be acknowledged—rested in the autonomy of their lines, measurable by aesthetic co-ordinates alone. And in these men by whom Swann now found himself surrounded there was nothing, down to the monocles which many of them wore (and which previously would at the most have enabled Swann to say that so-and-so wore a monocle) which, no longer restricted to the general connotation of a habit, the same in all of them, did not now strike him with a sense of individuality in each. Perhaps because he regarded General de Froberville and the Marquis de Bréauté, who were talking to each other just inside the door, simply as two figures in a picture, whereas they were the old and useful friends who had put him up for the Jockey Club and had supported him in duels, the General's monocle, stuck between his eyelids like a shell-splinter in his vulgar, scarred and overbearing face, in the middle of a forehead which it dominated like the single eye of the Cyclops, appeared to Swann as a monstrous wound which it might have been glorious to receive but which it was indecent to expose, ...*❞[4]

Princesse Alexandre Bibesco

A virtuoso pianist who had known Liszt, Wagner, and Gounod, Princesse Alexandre Bibesco was also the mother of Proust's friends Antoine and Émmanuel Bibesco, whom the novelist met when he was introduced into the Bibesco salon through the Princess's niece, the poet Anna de Noailles, and her brother, Constantin de Brancovan. Antoine remained a loyal and devoted friend to the end of Proust's life. Equally loyal, but in his own way, Proust offered to go to Roumania to console Antoine after his mother died on the family estate, but only if Bibesco would guarantee that there would be no flowers to arouse an attack of asthma. [1]

The Artists'
and
Writers' Way

Paul Desjardins (1859–1940)

Desjardins was an occasional poet and a professor of philosophy at the École des Sciences Politiques. Proust attended his lectures, admired his writings, and discovered the works of Ruskin in a periodical edited by Desjardins, *Bulletin de l'union pour l'action morale*. "According to M. Paul Desjardins," Anatole France wrote in an attempt to describe the pedagogue's methods and point of view, "style is evil. And yet M. Paul Desjardins has style, which only shows how true it is that the human soul is an abyss of contradictions. In his present state of mind one must not ask him his opinion on such frivolous and profane subjects as literature. He does not criticize. He anathematizes without hatred. Pale and melancholy, he goes his way, sowing tender maledictions." Later, Desjardins founded a lay religious community in the medieval abbey of Pontigny near Auxerre, where invited groups would gather for ten days of discussion each summer. In 1910 Proust thought of joining the *decades*, as they were called, but went to the Grand Hotel instead.

In *Swann's Way* Legrandin quotes a poem by Desjardins and then adds: "Perhaps you have never read Paul Desjardins. Read him, my boy, read him; in these days he is converted, they tell me, into a preaching friar, but he used to have the most charming water-colour touch. . . . "[1]

In *Time Regained* Proust transposes the abbey from Pontigny to Normandy, where the Verdurins and their friends set up a similar retreat, but the Narrator makes fun of the pretentious experiment:

❛ . . . *Thereupon, the following summer, they returned, lodging a whole colony of artists in an old cloister which they rented for next to nothing, and which made an admirable mediaeval abode. And upon my word, as I listen to this woman who, in passing through so many social circles of real distinction, has nevertheless preserved in her speech a little of the freshness and freedom of language of a woman of the people, a language which shows you things with the colour which your imagination sees in them, my mouth waters at the life which she avows to me they lived down there, each one working in his cell and the whole party assembling before luncheon, in a drawing-room so vast that it had two fireplaces, for really intelligent conversation interspersed with parlour games, . . .* ❜[2]

Alphonse Daudet (1840–97)

Novelist, playwright, and close friend of Edmond de Goncourt, Alphonse Daudet was introduced to Proust by Reynaldo Hahn in the winter of 1894. After the dinner at Daudet's house, Mme Daudet told her son Lucien that she had just met "a charming young man called Marcel Proust, extraordinarily well-read and with beautiful manners."[1] Later, Lucien became one of Proust's most intimate friends. The implication that the relationship might be more than platonic appeared in an article written for *Le Journal* by the novelist Jean Lorrain. Proust thereupon challenged Lorrain to a duel with pistols. After two ineffective shots had been exchanged, all returned home avenged.

Alphonse Daudet was impressed by his son's friend and kept his letters in files reserved for correspondence from great men. In response to one of Proust's penetrating insights, Daudet remarked that the young man was "the devil himself." For his part, Proust considered the older writer in a class with Théophile Gautier and George Sand, recalling when, as a boy reading in the dining room at Illiers, he first discovered the works of Alphonse Daudet. "My fondest dreams when I was a child," Proust wrote in a note to thank Daudet for his kindness, "could not have held out a prospect as unlikely or as delightful as that of being so graciously received one day by the Master who even then inspired me with passionate respect."[2] When Daudet finally died, after long suffering from syphillis, Proust comforted Lucien and accompanied him to his father's lying-in-state.

Anatole France (1844–1924)
Bergotte

I n the summer of 1889, an eighteen-year-old Proust was introduced to the salon of Mme Arman de Caillavet. "You'll find instruction as well as amusement here," his hostess said in greeting, "it's just like a school prize book."[1] It was there that he met the writer Anatole France, then forty-five and marked by what Proust saw as "a red nose curled like a snail-shell and a goatee beard."[2] Even before transforming France into Bergotte in *Within a Budding Grove*, Proust had made him the model for *Jean Santeuil's* M. de Traves, a writer whose novels also mysteriously resemble one another.

After divorcing his difficult wife in 1893, France lived with Mme Arman, in an arrangement whereby they made love each morning in his bachelor apartment before walking to her house on Avenue Hoche for lunch. Even though he had been writing in her library all afternoon, France would walk into his mistress's drawing room at teatime and announce: "I happened to be passing your house, and couldn't resist the pleasure of laying my delighted homage at your feet."[3]   In *Remembrance of Things Past* the story is reenacted by M. de Norpois and Mme de Villeparisis.

Proust took the name Bergotte from the hero of France's tetralogy *L'Histoire contemporaine,* and in *Within a Budding Grove* he comments at length on France, whom he claims to have been the only novelist he admired in his youth. When asked by Proust about his extraordinary production, France replied: "It's quite simple, my dear Marcel. When I was your age I wasn't good-looking and popular like you. So instead of going into society I stayed at home and did nothing but read."[4]

In *Within a Budding Grove* the Narrator reflects on France's fictional counterpart:

❛*Bergotte was sitting not far from me and I could hear quite clearly everything that he said. I understood then the impression that M. de Norpois had formed of him. He had indeed a peculiar "organ"; there is nothing that so alters the material qualities of the voice as the presence of thought behind what is being said: the resonance of the diphthongs, the energy of the labials are profoundly affected—as is the diction. His seemed to me to differ entirely from his way of writing, and even the things that he said from those with which he filled his books. But the voice issues from a mask behind which it is not powerful enough to make us recognise at first sight a face which we have seen uncovered in the speaker's literary style. At certain points in the conversation when Bergotte was in the habit of talking in a manner which not only M. de Norpois would have thought affected or unpleasant, it was a long time before I discovered an exact correspondence with the parts of his books in which his form became so poetic and so musical. At those points he could see in what he was saying a plastic beauty independent of whatever his sentences might mean, and as human speech reflects the human soul, though without expressing it as does literary style, Bergotte appeared almost to be talking nonsense, intoning certain words and, if he were pursuing, beneath them, a single image, stringing them together uninterruptedly on one continuous note, with a wearisome monotony. So that a pretentious, turgid and monotonous delivery was a sign of the rare aesthetic value of what he was saying, and an effect, in his conversation, of the same power which, in his books, produced that harmonious flow of imagery . . .*❜[5]

Claude Monet (1840–1926)
Elstir

Proust first admired the paintings of Claude Monet in the rotunda drawing room of his friend Mme Straus. There, on the elegant walls of the Boulevard Haussmann house, Monet's art hung side by side with 18th-century paintings by Nattier and Quentin de La Tour. Prince Edmond de Polignac, another friend, owned a Monet study of a tulip field painted near Haarlem. The novelist also saw the artist's work at the Durand-Ruel Gallery. In the preface to *La Bible d'Amiens*, Proust refers to the constantly changing colors of the cathedral's stone, like those which Monet "fixes in his sublime oils." So it was from direct experience that he could have Mme de Cambremer hold a discourse on the Impressionist's paintings and use Monet as an important reference for the character of Elstir, the painter in *Remembrance of Things Past*.

The Narrator recalls the discussion at Mme de Cambremer's after he had revealed his taste for Poussin, whereas his hostess had compared the seagulls in the sunset to the yellow waterlilies of Monet:

> ❝*In heaven's name," she exclaimed, "after a painter like Monet, who is quite simply a genius, don't go on and mention an old hack without a vestige of talent, like Poussin. I don't mind telling you frankly that I find him the deadliest bore. I mean to say, you cannot really call that sort of thing painting".*❞[1]

Elstir is a composite of a number of major painters active during the period. His race-course views suggest Degas and Manet, while Gustave Moreau could have supplied the gods and centaurs, and Renoir the beautiful bathing girls. Unquestionably, however, the cathedrals and the cliffs of Normandy are pure Monet. But, unlike most of the Impressionists, who wanted mainly to capture the optical reality of nature as perceived in light, Elstir went further, as George Painter has pointed out,[2] and explored "ambiguities" and metaphors:

> ❝ . . . *Naturally enough, what he had in his studio were almost all seascapes done here at Balbec. But I was able to discern from these that the charm of each of them lay in a sort of metamorphosis of the objects represented, analogous to what in poetry we call metaphor, and that, if God the Father had created things by naming them, it was by taking away their names or giving them other names that Elstir created them anew. The names which designate things correspond invariably to an intellectual notion, alien to our true impressions, and compelling us to eliminate from them everything that is not in keeping with that notion.*
> *Sometimes, at my window in the hotel at Balbec, in the morning when Françoise undid the blankets that shut out the light, or in the evening when I was waiting until it was time to go out with Saint-Loup, I had been led by some effect of sunlight to mistake what was only a darker stretch of sea for a distant coastline, or to gaze delightedly at a belt of liquid azure without knowing whether it belonged to sea or sky. But presently my reason would re-establish between the elements the distinction which my first impression had abolished. In the same way from my bedroom in Paris I would sometimes hear a dispute, almost a riot, in the street below, until I had traced back to*

its cause—a carriage for instance that was rattling towards me—that noise from which I now eliminated the shrill and discordant vociferations which my ear had really heard but which my reason knew that wheels did not produce. But the rare moments in which we see nature as she is, poetically, were those from which Elstir's work was created. One of the metaphors that occurred most frequently in the seascapes which surrounded him here was precisely that which, comparing land with sea, suppressed all demarcation between them. . . .[3]

Gabriel Fauré (1845–1924)
Vinteuil

Unable to contain the pleasure he received from Fauré's music, Proust wrote a fan letter to the composer, bursting forth: *"Monsieur, je n'aime, je n'adore pas seulement votre musique, j'en étais, j'en suis encore amoureux."*[1] The music of Fauré became interwoven with Proust's emotional life during the brief love affair the young writer had with Marie Finaly. "He and the charming Marie felt for one another a childish and reciprocated love," their mutual friend Fernand Gregh would later write, and Proust associated his affection for Marie with Fauré's setting of Baudelaire's "Chant d'automne."[2]

In a ribald reply to a critic who had called *Jean Santeuil* "a hotchpotch of litanies and lechery," Proust found other associations to make with the music of Gabriel Fauré. For lechery and litanies, he said, nothing was better than the composer's *Roman sans paroles*, "which is the sort of music a pederast might hum when raping a choir-boy."[3] As part of a composite made up of Debussy, Franck, d'Indy, and Saint-Saëns, Fauré figures significantly in the personality of Vinteuil, and certain themes of his Sonata for Piano and Violin can be heard in the Vinteuil Sonata.

In 1916 the Poulet Quartet was formed to present the chamber works of Franck, Chausson, Ravel, Borodin, and Fauré. At one of the ensemble's concerts, Proust asked the musicians if they would perform privately for him in his apartment on the Boulevard Haussmann. They agreed, and a few evenings later, at midnight, the fur-coated novelist mysteriously arrived at the apartment of Amable Massis, the Poulet's violist, and demanded that he forthwith marshal the other players for the private concert they had promised him. Following a supper of champagne and fried potatoes, supplied by the faithful Céleste, Proust had the program proceed in his famous bedroom, its dust-stained cork walls transforming the space into an acoustical chamber. The strange performance, although dominated by César Franck's work, also included Fauré's Piano Quartet.

Proust made music an important element in his novel, and out of deep personal appreciation, he handled it with great sensitivity. After hearing a Vinteuil piece for piano and violin played at Mme Verdurin's soirée, Swann contemplates the experience:

❝ . . . *At first he had appreciated only the material quality of the sounds which those instruments secreted. And it had been a source of keen pleasure when, below the delicate line of the violin-part, slender but robust, compact and commanding, he had suddenly become aware of the mass of the piano-part beginning to surge upward in plashing waves of sound, multiform but indivisible, smooth yet restless, like the deep blue tumult of the sea, silvered and charmed into a minor key by the moonlight. But then at a certain moment, without being able to distinguish any clear outline, or to give a name to what was pleasing him, suddenly enraptured, he had tried to grasp the phrase or harmony—he did not know which—that had just been played and that had opened and expanded his soul, as the fragrance of certain roses, wafted upon the moist air of evening, has the power of dilating one's nostrils. Perhaps it was owing to his ignorance of music that he had received so confused an impression, one of those that are nonetheless the only purely musical impressions, limited in their extent, entirely original, and irreducible to any other kind. An impression of this order, vanishing in an*

instant, is, so to speak, sine materia. *Doubtless the notes which we hear at such moments tend, according to their pitch and volume, to spread out before our eyes over surfaces of varying dimensions, to trace arabesques, to give us the sensation of breadth or tenuity, stability or caprice. But the notes themselves have vanished before these sensations have developed sufficiently to escape submersion under those which the succeeding or even simultaneous notes have already begun to awaken in us. And this impression would continue to envelop in its liquidity, its ceaseless overlapping, the motifs which from time to time emerge, barely discernible, to plunge again and disappear and drown, recognised only by the particular kind of pleasure which they instil, impossible to describe, to recollect, to name, ineffable—did not our memory, like a labourer who toils at the laying down of firm foundations beneath the tumult of the waves, by fashioning for us facsimiles of those fugitive phrases, enable us to compare and to contrast them with those that follow. And so, scarcely had the exquisite sensation which Swann had experienced died away, before his memory had furnished him with an immediate transcript, sketchy, it is true, and provisional, which he had been able to glance at while the piece continued, so that, when the same impression suddenly returned, it was no longer impossible to grasp. He could picture to himself its extent, its symmetrical arrangement, its notation, its expressive value; he had before him something that was no longer pure music, but rather design, architecture, thought, and which allowed the actual music to be recalled. . . . ♪*[4]

Claude Debussy (1862–1918)
Vinteuil

Suddenly seized by a craving for music, Proust in the winter of 1911 subscribed to a new telephonic invention that carried theater and opera performances over the telephone into the homes of subscribers. This was how the novelist heard Debussy's great masterpiece *Pelléas et Mélisande*, propped up in bed with the earpiece clamped to his ear, as the performance came over the Théâtrophone from the Opéra Comique. He was haunted by the music and continued to listen to performances on successive nights. In *Remembrance of Things Past* the Narrator claims to have experienced such a strong scent of roses at the point where Pelléas emerged from the cavern into the sea air that he suffered an asthma attack at every hearing. Given the character of his own delicate sensibility, Proust was wise to have remained safely in bed for his first "live" broadcast.

In his use of music, just as in the construction of his characters and places, Proust drew upon many sources. George Painter has identified the opening theme of the Vinteuil Septet, first heard at the Verdurins, with the seven-note tune, "like a mystical cock-crow an ineffable but over-shrill appeal to the eternal morning," that opens the Debussy Quartet.[1] On another occasion Proust would refer to the seven notes as "a summons to a supraterrestrial joy."[2]

Debussy, because of Reynaldo Hahn's dislike of his music, was suspicious of the Proust circle. After one of the few conversations they had together, the composer reported that he found Proust "long-winded and precious and a bit of an old woman."[3]

Édouard Risler (1873–1929)

At the first performance of Reynaldo Hahn's setting of Proust's *Portraits de peintres*, held at one of Madeleine Lemaire's Tuesdays in 1895, the accompanist was Édouard Risler. The pianist figured in Proust's musical life on other occasions, one of which was the "grand dinner" that the novelist gave at the Ritz in 1907 to honor his friend Gaston Calmette, editor of *Le Figaro*. The Duc de Guiche selected the food and wine, while Fauré was to have played. When the composer suddenly fell ill, Proust turned to Risler, who came forward and played Beethoven, Chopin, Couperin, and Fauré, all to the delight of the assembled guests. At Proust's special request, he also performed the piano transcriptions of the Overture to Wagner's *Meistersinger* and the *"Liebestod"* from *Tristan und Isolde*.

Marie de Heredia (1875–1963)

Proust was introduced into the family of the Parnassian poet José-Maria de Heredia in the winter of 1893. On Saturdays at the Heredia apartment in the Rue Balzac, a literary crowd would gather in one smoke-filled room, while the host's three beautiful daughters reigned over their own group in another. Proust preferred the company of the sisters, although he probably met Pierre Louÿs, André Gide, Henri de Régnier, and Paul Valéry in their father's study.

Marie de Heredia married Régnier and later became the cause of a duel between her husband and Robert de Montesquiou. This bizarre affair began when Mme de Régnier made an uncomplimentary reference to Montesquiou's celebrated cane, declaring it strong enough to hit several women without breaking. Régnier himself then added that the Count would look better with a fan. Montesquiou replied that he preferred swords. The duel took place before a fashionable audience in the Bois, with comic results but, fortunately, no injuries. Montesquiou later said that he had given better parties.[1]

Réjane (1857–1920)
Berma

Gabrielle-Charlotte Réju, or Réjane as she was known to the world at large, rivaled Sarah Bernhardt as the foremost actress of Belle Époque France, and together the two great ladies of the theater gave Proust his inspiration for the personality of Berma. The author was seventeen when, on the opening night of *Germinie Lacerteux*, he first saw Réjane on the stage. Even in his wildest adolescent fantasies, never could the young Proust have imagined that he would one day occupy the actress's house in the Rue Laurent-Pichat or re-create her personality in one of his fictional characters.

Réjane's son Jacques Porel, who in 1911 had seen Proust crossing the golf course at Cabourg dressed in a violet cape, would force his mother to read *Swann's Way* when it finally appeared in 1914. Upon hearing of his young admirer, Proust sent Céleste round to check him out. In reporting back, she described him as likable but "a bit flighty." When Porel came to call, Proust asked Céleste to close all the windows so that M. Porel "will not fly away."[1]

Porel and Proust became good friends, and after the Great War, which had left Porel a semi-invalid, Réjane invited Proust to take an apartment in her house, where Porel, his wife, and their seven-month-old daughter also lived. Then sixty-two, the actress was dying in her rooms on the second floor, although in 1920 she made a brief return to the stage in Henri Bataille's *La Vierge folle*. Shortly thereafter she also appeared in a film, which literally finished her career, since she died of exhaustion.

On the day that Proust moved to Réjane's house he also received the first proofs of *The Guermantes Way*. In this section of the novel the Narrator recalls the trauma of his family's move to a new apartment in the Guermantes mansion:

> ❛The twittering of the birds at daybreak sounded insipid to Françoise. Every word uttered by the maids upstairs made her jump; disturbed by all their running about, she kept asking herself what they could be doing. In other words, we had moved. . . .❜[2]

In *Time Regained* the ancient actress Berma virtually commits suicide for the benefit of her greedy daughter and son-in-law by throwing herself into a revival of *Phèdre*. It is the tragedy of the Rue Laurent-Pichat, only thinly disguised (and totally unrelated to the decent, filially devoted Porel), with the name of Réjane mentioned merely as a ruse intended to mislead suspicious readers:

> ❛. . . Berma, who suffered from a deadly disease which had obliged her to cut down her social activities to a minimum, had seen her condition deteriorate when, in order to pay for the luxurious existence which her daughter demanded and her son-in-law, ailing and idle, was unable to provide, she had returned to the stage. She knew that she was shortening her days, but she wanted to give pleasure to her daughter, to whom she handed over the large sums that she earned, and to a son-in-law whom she detested but flattered—for she feared, knowing that his wife adored him, that if she, Berma, did not do what he wanted, he might, out of spite, deprive her of the happiness of seeing her child. This child, with whom secretly the doctor who looked after her husband was in love, had allowed herself to be persuaded that these performances in Phèdre *were not really dangerous for her mother. . . . Have we not all seen an elderly riding-master with a weak heart go through a whole series of acrobatics which one would not have supposed his heart could stand for a single minute? Berma in the same way was an old campaigner of the stage, to the requirements of which her organs had so perfectly adapted themselves that she was able, by deploying her energies with a prudence invisible to the public, to give an illusion of good health troubled only by a purely nervous and imaginary complaint. . . . So that the poor mother, seriously engaged in her intimate dialogue with the death that was already installed within her, was compelled to get up early in the morning and drag herself out of the house. Nor was this enough. At about this time Réjane, in the full blaze of her talent, made some appearances on the stage in foreign countries which had an enormous success, and the son-in-law decided that Berma must not allow herself to be put in the shade; determined that his own family should pick up some of the same easily acquired glory, he forced his mother-in-law to set out on tours on which she was obliged to have injections of morphine, which might at any moment have killed her owing to the condition of her kidneys.* ❜[3]

Sarah Bernhardt (1844–1923)
Berma

Ranking the actresses of the Comédie Française, the theater that claimed Proust's greatest loyalty, Marcel the Narrator places Sarah Bernhardt first and then, immediately thereafter, Berma, the fictional actress composed of both Bernhardt and Réjane. By mentioning Bernhardt, Proust subtly managed to distance the real actress from the invented character of Berma, even though Bernhardt could be readily recognized in the Berma personality.

Like Bernhardt, Berma would revive old roles and present them for her public "as museum pieces":

❛ *. . . She was conscious, then, that certain roles have an interest which survives the novelty of their first production or the success of a revival; she regarded them, when interpreted by herself, as museum pieces which it might be instructive to set once more before the eyes of the generation which had admired her in them long ago, or of the one which had never yet seen her in them. . . .* ❜[1]

Truth to tell, I set little store by this opportunity of seeing and hearing Berma which, a few years earlier, had plunged me in such a state of agitation. And it was not without a sense of melancholy that I registered to myself my indifference to what at one time I had put before health, comfort, everything. It was not that there had been any diminution in my desire to be able to contemplate at first hand the precious particles of reality which my imagination envisioned. But it no longer located them in the diction of a great actress; since my visits to Elstir, it was on to certain tapestries, certain modern paintings that I transferred the inner faith I had once had in the acting, the tragic art of Berma; my faith and my desire no longer coming forward to pay incessant worship to the diction and the presence of Berma, the "double" that I possessed of them in my heart had gradually shrivelled, like those other "doubles" of the dead in ancient Egypt which had to be fed continually in order to maintain their originals in eternal life. That art had become a poor and pitiable thing. It was no longer inhabited by a deep-rooted soul.[2]

Gaston Calmette (1854–1914)

The dedication of *Swann's Way* is "To Monsieur Gaston Calmette as a testimony in profound and affectionate remembrance." It was probably around 1900 that Proust had been introduced to the gifted, sensitive editor of *Le Figaro* by Léon Daudet, and from that time until his death in 1914, Calmette published many articles by Proust. After the dinner he gave in honor of his mentor, Proust wrote to Mme Straus: "I planned a dinner solely out of compliment to Calmette, who is very nice to take my long articles, which are so little to the public taste."[1] Later, the novelist translated some of these experimental pastiches into the narrative of *Remembrance of Things Past*. One of them is Swann's obituary written in the proper *Figaro* style:

We learn with deep regret that M. Charles Swann passed away yesterday at his residence in Paris after a long and painful illness. A Parisian whose wit was widely appreciated, a discriminating but steadfastly loyal friend, he will be universally mourned, not only in those literary and artistic circles where the rare discernment of his taste made him a willing and a welcome guest, but also at the Jockey Club of which he was one of the oldest and most respected members. He belonged also to the Union and the Agricole. He had recently resigned his membership of the Rue Royale. His witty and striking personality never failed to arouse the interest of the public at all the great events of the musical and artistic seasons, notably at private views, where he was a regular attendant until the last few years, when he rarely left his house. The funeral will take place, etc.[2]

Louisa de Mornand (1884–1963)
Rachel

An actress of small talent, Louisa de Mornand gave Proust his model for Saint-Loup's mistress, the actress Rachel. She was in fact the mistress of Proust's friend the Marquis d'Albufera, whom the novelist served as go-between in his affair with Mornand throughout the summer and autumn of 1903. "Your remembrance is precious to me and I thank you," Proust wrote her in a flight of hyperbole during his tenure as love's messenger:

❝ . . . *How I would love to stroll with you in those streets of Blois, which must be a charming setting for your beauty. An old setting, a Renaissance setting. But also a new one, since I have never seen you in it. And in new places those we are fond of seem to us in a sense renewed. To see your lovely eyes reflect the soft-hued sky of Touraine, your exquisite form in profile against the old château would move me more than seeing you in a different gown, wearing different jewels. Side by side with the delicate embroideries of certain blue or pink dresses that you wear so well, I would like to test the effect of the fine stone embroideries that the old château also wears with a grace which for being rather old is no less becoming. . . .* ❞[1]

As often happened in his relations with women loved by his male friends, Proust conceived a romantic passion for Louisa de Mornand and even went so far as to inscribe to her a copy of his Ruskin translation, *La Bible d'Amiens*, with this couplet: "He who Louisa cannot win/No refuge has but Onan's sin." Long after her rupture with Albufera, Louisa de Mornand remained close to Proust, actually to the end of his life. Later she wrote: "Our was an *amitié amoureuse* in which there was no element of a banal flirtation or of an exclusive liaison, but on Proust's side a strong passion tinged with affection and desire, and on mine an attachment that was more than comradeship and really touched my heart."[2]

In *The Guermantes Way* Proust analyzes his own fantasy in a passage devoted to Rachel's power to create an illusion of beauty:

❝ *But the beginning of the afternoon's entertainment interested me in quite another way. It made me realise in part the nature of the illusion of which Saint-Loup was a victim with regard to Rachel, and which had set a gulf between the images that he and I respectively had of his mistress, when we saw her that morning among the blossoming pear trees. Rachel had scarcely more than a walking-on part in the little play. But seen thus, she was another woman. She had one of those faces to which distance—and not necessarily that between stalls and stage, the world being merely a larger theatre— gives form and outline and which, seen from close to, crumble to dust. Standing beside her one saw only a nebula, a milky way of freckles, of tiny spots, nothing more. At a respectable distance, all this ceased to be visible and, from cheeks that withdrew, were reabsorbed into her face, there rose like a crescent moon a nose so fine and so pure that one would have liked to be the object of Rachel's attention, to see her again and again, to keep her near one, provided that one had never seen her differently and at close range. . . .* ❞[3]

Méry Laurent
Odette

Reynaldo Hahn, in 1907, introduced Proust into the salon of the cocotte Méry Laurent at her villa "Les Talus," a rustic, charming little house on the edge of the Bois de Boulogne. Married at the age of fifteen to Claude Laurent, a bankrupt grocer, Méry left him seven months later with no support beyond her abilities as a model, entertainer, and eventually an actress. Near the end of the 1870s, Mme Laurent became the mistress of the American dentist Dr. Thomas Evans, who had helped the Empress Eugénie escape from the Tuileries Palace at the fall of the Second Empire. Her passion for poets and painters led her to Édouard Manet, whom she served as both model and mistress. After the death of Manet in 1883, Mme Laurent entered into a relationship with his friend, the poet Mallarmé.

Something of Méry Laurent's house, taste, and personality, all with their touch of vulgarity, lingers in Proust's portrait of Odette, who too had been a Second Empire courtesan. Like Mme Laurent, Odette succumbed to the new passion for *japonisme*:

❝ . . . *He fully realised that she was not intelligent. When she said how much she would like him to tell her about the great poets, she had imagined that she would immediately get to know whole pages of romantic and heroic verse, in the style of the Vicomte de Borelli, only even more moving. As for Vermeer of Delft, she asked whether he had been made to suffer by a woman, if it was a woman who had inspired him, and once Swann had told her that no one knew, she had lost all interest in that painter. She would often say: "Poetry, you know—well, of course, there'd be nothing like it if it was all true, if the poets really believed what they say. But as often as not you'll find there's no one so mean and calculating as those fellows. I know something about it: I had a friend, once, who was in love with a poet of sorts. In his verses he never spoke of anything but love and the sky and the stars. Oh! she was properly taken in! He had more than three hundred thousand francs out of her before he'd finished".* ❞[1]

Like Mme Laurent's house, the one lived in by Odette, with its clutter of bric-a-brac and "tasteful" arrangements, reflects its mistress's ideas of fashion and chic:

❝*From the ground floor, somewhat raised above street level, leaving on the left Odette's bedroom, which looked out to the back over another little street running parallel with her own, he had climbed a staircase that went straight up between dark painted walls hung with Oriental draperies, strings of Turkish beads, and a huge Japanese lantern suspended by a silken cord (which last, however, so that her visitors should not be deprived of the latest comforts of Western civilisation, was lighted by a gas-jet inside), to the two drawing-rooms, large and small. . . . Odette had received him in a pink silk dressing-gown, which left her neck and arms bare. She had made him sit down beside her in one of the many mysterious little alcoves which had been contrived in the various recesses of the room, sheltered by enormous palms growing out of pots of Chinese porcelain, or by screens upon which were fastened photographs and fans and bows of ribbon. . . .*❞[2]

Julia Bartet (1854–1941)

Vigorous rival of Sarah Bernhardt at the Comédie Française, Julia Bartet was invited, as were other well-known actresses, to give a reading of the poems of Robert de Montesquiou at one of Mme Lemaire's Tuesdays, where Proust first met the Count. At his own magnificent fête in the Pavillon Montesquiou, Mlle Bartet again recited some of the nobleman's verse to an even larger and more fashionable audience. It was on this occasion, in May 1894, that Proust had his first introduction to some of the Faubourg Saint-Germain's most brilliant hostesses. The novelist-to-be had arrived at the penultimate moment in his climb to the altitudinous Guermantes Way.

Lucie Delarue-Mardus (1880–1945)

Early in the twentieth century a small band of charming women became known for their talents and for the fact that, in the words of George Painter, they "preferred their own society to that of men." The leaders of this circle, which would act as a creative, leavening force in the stuffy, moribund society of prewar Europe, included Natalie Clifford Barney, Lucie Delarue-Mardus, Renée Vivien, and her friend Evelina Palmer. Writers such as Anna de Noailles and Colette enjoyed their company, and even Proust's married friend the Marquise de Clermont-Tonnerre, *née* Élisabeth de Gramont, found them more sympathetic than her unsatisfactory husband. As one member of the sisterhood remarked to Montesquiou: "People call it unnatural—all I can say is, it's always come naturally to me!"[1]

Mme Delarue-Mardus was married to the sinister Dr. Mardus, translator of *Arabian Nights*, a copy of which Proust's Narrator receives from his mother, who would later regret having made the gift. Mme Delarue-Mardus was devoted to Natalie Barney, "the pure and

faithful companion whose pride, loyalty and greatness I esteem so highly," and made the famous American *amazone* the heroine of her novel *L'Ange et les pervers*, "where I have described and analysed at full length both Natalie and the life into which she initiated me, in which it was not until much later than I ceased to play more than the sexless role of the angel!"[2]

In his consideration of the origins, causes, and permutations of homosexuality, Proust explores the relationships between a number of the women in *Remembrance of Things Past* who experienced or pursued a variety of inclinations. Mlle Vinteuil's relationship with her female friend, for example, is "one of those situations wrongly believed to be the exclusive appanage of bohemian life; such situations are produced each time a vice which Nature herself causes to appear in a child (sometimes only by mixing the virtues of the father and mother, as She might mix the colors of their eyes) needs to reserve for itself the situation and security which are necessary for its development."[3]

The possibility of a hidden meaning in Albertine's association with such "practicing and professional" Sapphists as Mlle Vinteuil and her friend engulfs the Narrator in confusion and hopeless wonderment. The secret lesbian world held mysteries that repeatedly attracted Proust and inspired some of his most vivid passages between memory and fantasy, and the inquiries he makes in the narrative of *Remembrance of Things Past* no doubt grew out of his awareness of the sexual complexities and ambiguities that existed within society itself.

Cora Laparcerie (1875–1951)

During the late 1890s Proust and his mother would frequently organize a "grand dinner at 9 Boulevard Malesherbes" and use the occasion to lionize carefully selected artists and literary figures. At one of these affairs in 1899, given in honor of Robert de Montesquiou, Anatole France, and Anna de Noailles, Proust invited the actress Cora Laparcerie to recite verses by each of the poet-guests. At another gathering, Proust had Sarah Bernhardt, through an arrangement made by Reynaldo Hahn, give a reading of Anna de Noailles's poems, a recitation guaranteed to bring the host a certain social notoriety. At a dinner honoring Mme de Noailles, Proust had the tables decorated with bouquets of the wild flowers mentioned in the verses read by Bernhardt, another theatrical touch that impressed the fashionable guests. A few days later Proust wrote to the poet:

❝ *I was awaiting your poems with the anxious certainty of one who knows he will have new beauty to admire. I was as sure of that as the prince in the fairy tale, for whom the bees who worked and made the rose bushes bloom, was sure of having honey and roses. . . .*

I thank you for letting these verses alight for an evening like those pigeons which walk in procession this evening but which once stopped to rest at the edge of your sandals. . . .❞ [1]

Paul Nadar (1856–1939)

By the time of Proust's birth in 1871, the name Nadar was already famous in Paris, thanks to the journalist and caricaturist Félix Nadar, who had established his photographic studio in 1853–54, hardly fifteen years after the invention of photography. In 1859, when Nadar first photographed the young Jewish actress Sarah Bernhardt, his reputation was already secure among the "Who's Who" of French arts, letters, and fashions. Dumas *père*, George Sand, Manet, Courbet, Rossini, Offenbach, Gautier, and the brothers Goncourt typified the period's great who sat to have their photographic portraits made by Félix Nadar.

After first working in the Rue Saint-Lazare, Nadar moved his studio to a more fashionable address on the Boulevard des Capucines, where the sign, emblazoned across the façade in a distinctive script, became one of the busy thoroughfare's best-known landmarks. Victor Hugo had only to write "Nadar" on a stamped envelope for the missive to be delivered.

Nadar's portraits must be counted among the greatest in the history of photography. Direct, forceful, and revealing as they are, the pictures never seem definitive, for their very spontaneity implies other possibilities for exploring the sitter's character. Like most great portraitists, Nadar seems instinctively to have avoided synthesis—that impression of closed completeness—in favor of a fleeting yet focused image, an image that gives his work its singular quality.

Félix's son Paul began to take over the Nadar atelier around 1880, when the firm moved again, this time to the Rue d'Anjou, and Félix had begun to make plans to retire from the Paris scene. Paul, despite the commercial tone of his work, continued to attract an enormous following from both artistic and fashionable Paris. Claude Monet, for example, had his portrait made in 1889, some two decades after he, as an obscure, sometimes reviled, painter had become an intimate of the artistic circle that regularly met at Félix's studio. And it was in this very studio that in 1874 Monet and his friends—Renoir, Degas, Cézanne, Pissarro, Sisley—planned and opened the historic first Impressionist exhibition, mounted by the painters themselves when it became evident they could never gain access to the official Salon, the channel through which French artists had always sold or promoted their works.

Given the fame of the Nadar studio and the conspicuous place it had gained in Parisian life—by holding a mirror up to that society in hundreds of portraits photographed throughout the 1870s and 1880s—we should not be surprised that the Proust family, like so many of their friends and connections, went to Nadar to have their appearances documented.

In *Contre Sainte-Beuve* Proust compares the faces of famous people with historic buildings, only to conclude that in both "what we see . . . is less than what we imagined." Something of the same disappointment may occur when we compare the portraits of Paul Nadar to the transformation worked upon their subjects in *Remembrance of Things Past*. With a face, as with a famous historic building, "our first impression . . . is determined by a feature which the descriptions we've heard before and generally say nothing about. As what strikes us at first sight in a celebrity known by hearsay will be his face crinkles when he laughs or something slightly silly about his mouth, or a clumsy nose or sloping shoulders. . . . "[1]

It goes without saying, of course, that the straightforward, composed record compiled by Paul Nadar cannot be compared to the profound portraits built up layer by psychological layer through the imagination of Proust the writer. Yet the images drawn from the photographer's files, for all their subterfuges of pose, costume, disguised crinkle, and stiff studio setting, do at least suggest the raw material of physiognomy, dress, and personality out of which Proust created his imaginary world.

Notes

Introduction
1. George Painter, *Marcel Proust* (Vintage, 1978), II, p. 249; 2. Céleste Albaret, *Monsieur Proust*, trans. by Barbara Bray (Collins, 1976), p. 257; 3. Marcel Proust, *The Captive* (Vintage, 1981), p. 199; 4. Alistair Horne, *The Fall of Paris* (St. Martin's, 1965), p. 372; 5. Edmond de Goncourt, *Paris under Siege: 1870–1871*, trans. by George Becker (Cornell U., 1969), p. 303; 6. Marcel Proust, *Within a Budding Grove* (Vintage, 1981), p. 527; 7. Marcel Proust, *Swann's Way* (Vintage, 1981), p. 462; 8. Howard Moss, *The Magic Lantern of Marcel Proust* (Nonpareil, 1963), p. 124; 9. Marcel Proust, *Time Regained* (Vintage, 1981), p. 843; 10. Roger Shattuck, *Marcel Proust* (Princeton U., 1974), p. 7; 11. Painter, *op. cit.*, p. xiii; 12. Mina Curtiss, *Other People's Letters: A Memoir* (Houghton-Mifflin, 1978), p. 44; 13. Élisabeth de Clermont-Tonnerre, *Pomp and Circumstance*, trans. by Brian Downs (J. Cape & H. Smith, 1929), pp. 15–16; 14. Curtiss, *op. cit.*, p. 47; 15. Nigel Gosling, *Nadar* (New York, 1976), p. 11; 16. Philip Kolb, ed., *Marcel Proust: Selected Letters: 1880–1903*, trans. by Ralph Mannheim with intros. by J.M. Cocking (Doubleday, 1983), p. 50; 17. *Swann's Way*, p. 318; 18. *Within a Budding Grove*, p. 820; 19. Albaret, *op. cit.*, pp. 174–175; 20. Marthe Bibesco, *The Veiled Wanderer: Marcel Proust*, trans. by Roland Grant (Falcon, 1949), p. 42; 21. Marcel Proust, *The Guermantes Way* (Vintage, 1981), p. 49–50; 22. *Swann's Way*, pp. 72–73; 23. Painter, *op. cit.*, II, p. 286; 24. Walter Benjamin, *Illuminations* (Schocken, 1969), p. 211; 25. *The Guermantes Way*, pp. 371–372; 26. *Swann's Way*, p. 196.

Mme Adrien Proust
1. Albaret, *op. cit.*, p. 142; 2. *Ibid.*, p. 139; 3. *Within a Budding Grove*, pp. 843–844; 4. *Swann's Way*, pp. 37–38; 5. *Ibid.*, pp. 39–40.

Robert Proust
1. Albaret, *op. cit.*, p. 169; 2. *Ibid.*; 3. Painter, *op. cit.*, I, p. 381.

Mme Émile Straus
1. Mina Curtiss, *Letters of Marcel Proust* (Random House, 1949), pp. 21–22; 2. *Ibid.*, p. 388.

Charles Haas
1. *Swann's Way*, p. 229; 2. *Ibid.*, p. 221; 3. *Ibid.*, pp. 16–19.

Gabriel Hanotaux
1. *Within a Budding Grove*, pp. 486–489.

Mme Aubernon de Nerville
1. Painter, *op. cit.*, I, p. 98; 2. *Ibid.*, pp. 228–229; 3. *Ibid.*, p. 100.

Dr. Samuel Pozzi
1. Painter, *op. cit.*, I, pp. 125–126; 2. *Swann's Way*, pp. 217–218.

Professor Georges Dieulafoy
1. *The Guermantes Way*, pp. 354–355.

Madeleine Lemaire
1. *The Captive*, pp. 250–253; 2. *Swann's Way*, p. 206.

Camille Barrère
1. Painter, *op. cit.*, I, p. 329; 2. Kolb, ed., *op. cit.*, p. 228; 3. *Within a Budding Grove*, p. 471; 4. *Ibid.*, pp. 495–496.

Reynaldo Hahn
1. William Sansom, *Proust and His World* (Thames & Hudson, 1973), p. 57; 2. Painter, *op. cit.*, I, p. 214; 3. *Swann's Way*, p. 238.

Jeanne Pouquet
1. Painter, *op. cit.*, I, p. 82; 2. *Swann's Way*, pp. 153–154.

Willie Heath
1. Painter, *op. cit.*, I, p. 124; 2. *Ibid.*

Laure Hayman
1. Painter, *op. cit.*, I, p. 87; 2. J.E. Rivers, *Proust and the Art of Love* (Columbia U., 1980), p. 47; 3. Kolb, ed., *op. cit.*, p. 39; 4. *Swann's Way*, p. 213; 5. *Within a Budding Grove*, pp. 663–664.

Nicolas Cottin
1. Painter, *op. cit.*, II, p. 160; 2. *Ibid.*

Alfred Agostinelli
1. Rivers, *op. cit.*, pp. 89–90; 2. *Ibid.*, p. 90

Marie de Benardaky
1. *Within a Budding Grove*, p. 528.

Mme de Benardaky
1. Painter, *op. cit.*, I, p. 48; 2. *Within a Budding Grove*, pp. 638–639.

Lt. Comte Armand de Cholet
1. Painter, *op. cit.*, I, p. 74; 2. *Within a Budding Grove*, pp. 785–786, 791.

Comtesse Élisabeth Greffulhe
1. Kolb, ed., *op. cit.*, p. 51; 2. *Ibid.*, pp. 50–51; 3. Mina Curtiss, *Other People's Letters*, p. 172; 4. Curtiss, *Other People's Letters*, p. 176; 5. *The Guermantes Way*, pp. 384–385.

Comtesse Laure de Chevigné
1. Swann's Way, pp. 193–194.

Duc Armand de Guiche
1. Painter, *op. cit.*, I, p. 316.

Marquis Boni de Castellane
1. *Within a Budding Grove*, pp. 783–784.

Marquise Boni de Castellane
1. Painter, *op. cit.*, II, p. 105

Vicomte Robert d'Humières
1. *Time Regained*, pp. 877–878.

Comte Henri Greffulhe
1. *The Guermantes Way*, pp. 25–27.

Comte Robert de Montesquiou
1. Painter, *op. cit.*, I, p. 128; 2. *Ibid.*, p. 131. Whistler's portrait of Montesquiou now hangs in the Frick collection in New York City; 3. *Ibid.*; 4. Marcel Proust, *Cities of the Plain* (Vintage, 1981), pp. 973–974.

Prince Boson de Sagan
1. *Time Regained*, pp. 891–892.

Comte Louis de Turenne
1. Painter, *op. cit.*, I, p. 185; 2. *The Guermantes Way*, pp. 445–446.

Costume Ball of the Princesse de Léon
1. Painter, *op. cit.*, I, p. 160; 2. *The Captive*, pp. 28–29.

Marquise de Brantes
1. Kolb, ed., *op. cit.*, p. 168; 2. Painter, *op. cit.*, I, p. 177.

Princesse Mathilde
1. *Within a Budding Grove*, pp. 583–584.

Edward, Prince of Wales
1. Olivier Dabescat was the former maître d'hôtel at the Paris Ritz, suggesting that the hotel had become the royal château at Saint-Cloud; 2. Mme Standish had been the mistress of the Prince of Wales, and the Ritz was her favorite hotel; 3. Bibesco, *op. cit.*

Princesse Hélène Soutzo
1. Painter, *op. cit.*, II, p. 254; 2. *Ibid.*, p. 170; 3. *Time Regained*, p. 863.

Prince Constantin Radziwill
1. Painter, *op. cit.*, I, p. 188; 2. *Ibid.*, p. 387; 3. *Ibid.*, p. 262; 4. *Time Regained*, p. 996–997.

General Marquis Gaston de Galliffet
1. Painter, *op. cit.*, I, p. 239; 2. *Ibid.*, p. 151; 3. *Ibid.*, p. 152; 4. *Swann's Way*, p. 335.

Princesse Alexandre Bibesco
1. Painter, *op. cit.*, I, p. 376.

Paul Desjardins
1. *Swann's Way*, p. 130; 2. *Time Regained*, pp. 732–733.

Alphonse Daudet
1. Painter, *op. cit.*, I, p. 186; 2. Kolb, ed., *op. cit.*, pp. 88–89.

Anatole France
1. Painter, *op. cit.*, I, p. 65; 2. *Ibid.*; 3. *Ibid.*, p. 68; 4. *Ibid.*, p. 70; 5.. *Within a Budding Grove*, p. 592.

Claude Monet
1. *Cities of the Plain*, pp. 839–840; 2. Painter, *op. cit.*, I, p. 280; 3. *Within a Budding Grove*, pp. 893–894.

Gabriel Fauré
1. Painter, *op. cit.*, I, p. 173; 2. *Ibid.*, p. 118; 3. *Ibid.*, II, p. 175; 4. *Swann's Way*, pp. 227–228.

Claude Debussy
1. Painter, *op. cit.*, II, p. 246; 2. *Ibid.*; 3. *Ibid.*, I, p. 291.

Marie de Heredia
1. Painter, *op. cit.*, I, p. 211–212.

Réjane
1. Painter, *op. cit.*, II, p. 289; 2. *The Guermantes Way*, p. 3; 3. *Time Regained*, pp. 1046–1048.

Sarah Bernhardt
1. *Within a Budding Grove*, p. 476–477; 2. *The Guermantes Way*, p. 32.

Gaston Calmette
1. Curtiss, *Letters*, p. 171; 2. *The Captive*, p. 198.

Louisa de Mornand
1. Kolb, ed., *op. cit.*, pp. 337–338;

2. Painter, *op. cit.*, II, pp. 12–13; 3. *The Guermantes Way*, pp. 177–178.

Méry Laurent
1. *Swann's Way*, p. 263; 2. *Ibid.*, p. 240.

Lucie Delarue-Mardus
1. Painter, *op. cit.*, II, p. 327–328; 2. *Ibid.*, p. 328; 3. *Rivers*, *op. cit.*, p. 159.

Cora Laparcerie
1. Kolb, ed., *op. cit.*, pp. 219–220.

Paul Nadar
1. Sylvia Townsend Warner, trans., *Proust on Art and Literature: 1896–1919* (New York, 1956), p. 246.

Index

Italics identify fictional characters in the Proustian world or the titles of books written by Marcel Proust.

Agostinelli, Alfred (*Albertine*): 52–53
Agostinelli, Émile: 52–53
Albaret, Céleste: 8, 14, 21, 24, 48, 64, 104, 111
Albaret, Odilon: 17
Albertine: 52, 122
Albufera, Marquis Louis d' (*Saint-Loup*): 66, 116
Alexandra, Queen: 80
Armand, Mme (see Caillavet, Mme Arman de)
Aubernon de Nerville, Lydie (*Mme Verdurin*): 33–34
Austen, Jane: 15

Balzac, Honoré de: 15
Barney, Natalie Clifford: 121
Barrère, Camille (*Norpois*): 40–41
Bartet, Julia: 120
Bataille, Henri: 111
Baudelaire, Charles: 104
Beethoven, Ludwig von: 108
Benardaky, Mme de (*Odette*): 58–59, 72
Benardaky, Marie de (*Gilberte*): 57–58
Benardaky, Nelly de: 57
Benardaky, Nicolas de: 57
Benedetti, Count: 85
Benjamin, Walter: 18
Bergotte: 101, 113
Berma: 110–111, 113, 114
Bernhardt, Sarah (*Berma*): 110, 112–113, 120, 122, 124
Bibesco, Princesse Alexandre: 94
Bibesco, Prince Antoine: 66, 94
Bibesco, Prince Emmanuel: 66, 94
Bisaccia, Duc de: 30
Bizet, Georges: 26
Bizet, Jacques: 26
Bizet-Straus, Geneviève (see Straus, Mme Émile)
Blacas, Duc de: 30
Blancard, Victor: 34
Blanche, Jacques-Émile (*Elstir*): 48
Borelli, Vicomte de: 119
Borodin, Aleksandr: 104
Bourget, Paul: 48

Brancovan, Constantin de: 94
Brantes, Marquis de: 18, 84
Bréauté-Consalvi, Marquis or Comte Hannibal: 80–81, 92
Breteuil, Comte Henri de (*Bréauté*): 30, 80
Brissac, Duc de: 70

Caillavet, Arman de: 11
Caillavet, Mme Arman de (*Mme Verdurin*): 11, 101
Calmette, Gaston: 26, 108, 114–115
Cambremer, Mme de: 102
Caraman-Chimay, Élisabeth de (see Greffuhle, Comtesse)
Castellane, Marquis Boni de (*Saint-Loup*): 16, 68–70, 81
Castellane, Marquise Boni de (neé Anna Gould): 69, 70
Cézanne, Paul: 124
Chambord, Comte de: 65
Charlus, Baron de: 7, 8, 10, 13, 16, 70, 71, 76, 79
Chausson, Ernest: 104
Chevigné, Comte Adhéaume de: 65
Chevigné, Comtesse Laure de (*Duchesse de Guermantes*): 64, 65–66
Cholet, Lt. Comte Armand de (*Saint-Loup*): 60–61
Chopin, Frédéric: 108
Clermont-Tonnerre, Duc de: 30
Clermont-Tonnerre, Duchesse de: 11, 12, 17
Colette: 121
Comédie Française: 12, 79, 113, 120
Cottard, Dr.: 34, 39
Cottin, Céline: 50
Cottin, Nicolas: 50–51
Couperin, François: 108
Courbet, Gustave: 124
Cours Pape-Carpentier: 26
Curtiss, Mina: 13, 62, 64

Dabescat, Olivier: 89
Daudet, Alphonse (*Bergotte*): 98–99
Daudet, Léon: 34, 114
Daudet, Lucien: 13, 47, 98
Debussy, Claude (*Vinteuil*): 43, 104, 106–107
Degas, Edgar: 26, 76, 102, 124

Delarue-Mardus, Lucie: 120–121
Desjardins, Paul: 97–98
Detaille, Édouard: 80, 81
Dickens, Charles: 15
Dieulafoy, Dr. Georges (*Cottard, Dieulafoy*): 36–37
Doré, Gustave: 12
Dreyfus, Alfred: 26, 34, 90, 92
Dumas, Alexandre: 12, 124
Dumas *fils*, Alexandre: 85, 86
Durand-Ruel Gallery: 102

Edward VII: 80, 86–87
Elstir: 13, 102–103, 114
d'Estissac, Duc: 30
Eugénie, Empress: 119
Evans, Dr. Thomas: 119

Faulkner, William: 14, 15
Fauré, Gabriel (*Vinteuil*): 43, 104–105
Finaly, Marie (*Albertine*): 52
Fitz-James, Comte Robert de: 79
Flaubert, Gustave: 85, 86
Flers, Comte Robert de: 13
Forain, Jean-Louis: 26, 76
France, Anatole (*Bergotte*): 11, 76, 97, 100–101, 122
Franck, César (*Vinteuil*): 104
Franco-Prussian War: 8, 92
Françoise: 17, 23, 102, 111
Froberville, General de: 92
Fürstenberg, Prince Karl Egon von: 48

Galliffet, General Marquis Gaston de (*Gen. de Froberville*): 8, 79, 92–93
Garnier, Charles: 9
Gautier, Théophile: 98, 124
Gide, André: 54, 109
Gilberte: 7, 57, 58, 72
Goncourt, Edmond de: 8, 9, 33, 76, 85, 98, 124
Gould, Anna (see Castellane, Marquise Boni de)
Gramont, Duc de: 11, 37, 76
Gramont, Duchesse de: 66
Gramont, Élisabeth de: 63, 121
Greffulhe, Comtesse Élisabeth (*Duchesse* and *Princesse de Guermantes*): 14, 62–64, 67, 80, 86
Greffulhe, Comte Henri: 62, 67, 74–75

Gregh, Fenand: 104
Guermantes, Duc de: 68, 75
Guermantes, Duchesse de: 14, 15, 16, 17, 18, 26, 62–64, 65, 66, 75, 80–81, 86
Guermantes, Prince de: 79, 90
Guermantes, Princesse de: 14, 15, 17, 62–63
Guiche, Duc Armand de (*Saint-Loup*): 14, 64, 66–67, 108
Guiche, Duchesse de: 14
Gyp (see Comtess de Martel)

Haas, Charles (*Swann*): 8, 28–30, 76, 79, 85, 86, 92
Hahn, Reynaldo: 42–43, 47, 84, 98, 107, 108, 119, 122
Hanotaux, Gabriel: 31–32
Hayman, Laure (*Odette*): 48–50, 58
Heath, Willie: 46–47
Heredia, José-Maria de: 109
Heredia, Marie de: 109
Hugo, Victor: 124
Humières, Vicomte Robert d' (*Saint-Loup*): 71–72

Ibsen, Henrik: 34
Indy, Vincent d' (*Vinteuil*): 104

James, Henry: 9, 16
Jockey Club: 15, 30, 60, 92, 114
Joyce, James: 15
Jupien: 79, 89

Keats, John: 11

La Gandara, Antoine: 62
Lamartine, Alphonse de: 72
Laparcerie, Cora: 122–123
La Rochefoucauld, 17, 76
La Rochefoucauld, Comte Aimery de (*Prince de Guermantes*): 30
Laszlo, 62
La Tour, Quentin de: 102
Lau, Marquis du: 30
Laurent, Méry (*Odette*): 118–119
Le Cuziat, Albert (*Jupien*): 16, 17
Legrandin: 16, 98
Lemaire, Madeleine (*Mme Verdurin*): 38–39, 43, 66, 69, 108, 120
Lemaître, Jules (*Bergotte*): 113
Léon, Princesse de: 81
Leonardo da Vinci: 47
Lévy, Calmann: 72
Liszt, Franz: 94
Lorrain, Jean: 98
Louÿs, Pierre: 109
Ludre, Comtesse de: 29–30

Malakoff, Mlle de: 58
Mallarmé, Stéphane: 76, 119
Manet, Édouard: 102, 119, 124
Mardus, Dr. Joseph: 121
Martel, Comtesse de (Gyp): 72–73
Massenet, Jules: 43
Massis, Amable: 104
Mathilde, Princesse: 16, 34, 85–86
Mazarine Library: 31
McCarthy, Mary: 15
Melville, Herman: 15
Mérimée, Prosper: 85
Mirabeau, Comte Honoré de: 72
Molière: 72
Monet, Claude (*Elstir*): 102–103, 124
Montesquiou, Robert de (*Baron de Char-*

lus): 7, 8, 13, 62, 64, 68, 76–77, 90, 109, 121, 122
Montmorency, Duc de: 30
Morand, Paul: 89
Moreau, Gustave: 76, 102
Mornand, Louisa de (*Rachel*): 116–117
Moss, Howard: 10, 18
Mouchy, Duc de: 30
Murat, Prince: 30

Nadar, Félix: 10, 12–13, 124
Nadar, Paul: 12, 13, 16, 18, 29, 38, 47, 52, 60, 62, 69, 75, 76, 80, 124–125
Napoleon I: 16, 85, 86
Napoleon III: 8, 86
Narrator: 7, 14, 16, 17, 21, 23–24, 30, 32, 40, 48, 58, 69, 70, 75, 85, 89, 98, 102, 107, 111, 113, 120, 121, 122
Nattier, Jean-Marc: 102
Nicholas II, Tsar of Russia: 32, 85
Nicolson, Harold: 16
Noailles, Comte de: 30
Noailles, Duc de: 30
Noailles, Comtesse Anna de: 66, 94, 121, 122
Norpois: 31, 32, 40, 101

Odette: 13, 26, 43, 48, 50, 58–59, 85–86, 119
Offenbach, Jacques: 10, 12, 124
d'Orléans, Duc: 48
d'Orléans, Duchesse: 86

Painter, George; 11, 76, 102, 107, 121
Palatine, Princess: 86
Palmer, Evelina: 121
Parme, Princesse de: 85
Pissarro, Camille: 124
Poix, Prince de: 30
Polignac, Edmond de: 8, 102
Porel, Jacques: 110–111
Potter, Paulus: 43
Pougy, Liane de: 7
Poulet Quartet: 104
Pourtalès, Comtesse Paul de: 30
Poussin, Nicolas: 102
Pozzi, Dr. Samuel (*Cottard*): 34–35, 85
Primoli, Count: 85
Proust, Dr. Adrien: 8, 21, 31
Proust, Mme Adrien: 13, 21–24, 40, 72
Proust, Marcel: *La Bible d'Amiens*, 102; *The Captive*, 7, 8; *Contre Sainte-Beuve*, 124; *The Guermantes Way*, 37, 80, 86, 111, 116; "Impressions de route en automobile," 52; *Jean Santeuil*, 58, 60, 101, 104; *Pastiches et mélanges*, 86; *Les Plaisirs et les jours*, 47, 60, 67; *Portraits de peintres*, 43, 108; *Remembrance of Things Past*, 7, 8, 9, 11, 12, 13, 15, 16, 18, 21, 23, 24, 26, 32, 43, 48, 50, 52, 54, 75, 85, 101, 102, 107, 122; *Swann's Way*, 19, 34, 92, 98, 110,, 114; *Time Regained*, 89, 90, 98, 111; *Within a Budding Grove*, 13, 32, 40, 60, 69, 101
Proust, Robert: 24–25

Rachel: 116
Racine: 113
Radziwill, Prince Constantin (*Prince de Guermantes*): 90–91
Radziwill, Prince Léon (*Saint-Loup*): 90
Radziwill, Prince Michel: 57
Ravel, Maurice (*Vinteuil*): 104
Régnier, Henri de: 109

Réjane (*Berma*): 110–111, 113
Renan, Ernest: 85
Renoir, Auguste: 102, 124
Risler, Édouard: 108
Ritz, hotel: 84, 89, 90, 108
Rochefort, Victor Henri: 12
Rohan-Chabot family: 76
Rohan-Chabot, Duc Alain de: 81
Rossini, Gioachino: 124
Rothschild, Baron Adolf de: 30
Rothschild, Baron Alphonse de: 26
Rothschild, Baron Edmond de: 26
Rothschild, Baron Gustave de: 26
Ruskin, John: 97

Sade, Laure de (see Chevigné, Comtesse Laure)
Sade, Marquis de: 65
Sagan, Prince Boson de: 70, 78–79, 92
Saint-Loup: 16, 21, 23, 60–61, 68–69, 71–72, 81, 102, 116
Saint-Saëns, Camille (*Vinteuil*): 43, 104
Saint-Simon, Duc de: 76, 89
Sainte-Beuve, Charles: 85, 86
Sainte-Euverte, Mme de: 79, 92
Sand, George: 98, 124
Sansom, William: 43
Sardou, Victorien: 12
Saxe, Maréchal de: 81
Schubert, Franz: 64
Schumann, Robert: 72
Sévigné, Mme de: 21
Shattuck, Robert: 10
Sisley, Alfred: 124
Soutzo, Princesse Hélène: 88, 89
Standish, Madame: 89
Straus, Émile: 26, 85
Straus, Mme Émile (*Duchesse de Guermantes*): 7, 8, 11, 26–27, 29, 85, 102, 114
Swann: 7, 8, 13, 29–30, 33, 43, 48, 50, 85–86, 92, 104, 107, 114, 119

Taine, Hippolyte: 85
Talleyrand-Périgord, Duc de: 68
Talleyrand-Périgord, Hélie de (see Sagan, Prince Boson de)
Theodosius II: 32
Tissot, James: 8, 92
Tolstoy, Leo: 15
Traves, M. de: 101
Turenne, Comte Louis de (*Bréauté*): 79, 80, 92

Valéry, Paul: 109
van Dyke, Anthony: 43, 47
Verdurin, Mme: 16, 33, 34, 38–39, 76, 98, 104, 107
Verlaine, Paul: 43, 76
Vermeer, Jan: 119
Victoria, Queen: 86
Villeparisis, Mme de: 17, 60, 64, 69, 70, 101
Vinteuil: 13, 104, 106, 107
Vinteuil, Mlle: 122
Vivien, Renée: 121

Wagner, Richard: 108
Wagram, Princesse Alexandre: 62
Watteau, Antoine: 43, 50
Weil, Jeanne (see Proust, Mme Adrien)
Weil, Louis: 8, 48
Whistler, James: 76
William II: 72
World War I: 9, 111